The Teacher-Researcher

The Teacher-Researcher

How to Study Writing in the Classroom

Miles Myers
Bay Area Writing Project
San Francisco

ERIC Clearinghouse on Reading and Communication Skills
National Institute of Education

National Council of Teachers of English
1111 Kenyon Road, Urbana, Illinois 61801

To Eugene McCreary, former master teacher and teacher-researcher at McChesney Junior High School, Oakland, California

NCTE Editorial Board: Candy Carter, Julie M. Jensen, Delores Lipscomb, John S. Mayher, Elisabeth McPherson, John C. Maxwell, *ex officio*, Paul O'Dea, *ex officio*

Staff Editor: Lee Erwin

Book Design: Tom Kovacs for TGK Design

NCTE Stock Number 50128

Published 1985 by the ERIC Clearinghouse on Reading and Communication Skills and the National Council of Teachers of English, 1111 Kenyon Road, Urbana, Illinois 61801. Printed in the United States of America.

This publication was prepared with funding from the National Institute of Education, U.S. Department of Education, under contract no. 400-83-0025. Contractors undertaking such projects under government sponsorship are encouraged to express freely their judgment in professional and technical matters. Prior to publication, the manuscript was submitted to the Editorial Board of the National Council of Teachers of English for critical review and determination of professional competence. This publication has met such standards. Points of view or opinions, however, do not necessarily represent the official view or opinions of either the National Council of Teachers of English or the National Institute of Education.

Library of Congress Cataloging in Publication Data

Myers, Miles.
The teacher-researcher

Bibliography: p.
Includes index.
"Contract no. 400-83-0025"—T.p. verso.
1. English language—Composition and exercises—
Evaluation.   2. Education—Research—Methodology.
I. Title.
LB1576.M95   1985   808'.042   85-15262
ISBN 0-8141-5012-8

Contents

Foreword

The Educational Resources Information Center (ERIC) is a national information system operated by the National Institute of Education (NIE) of the U.S. Department of Education. It provides ready access to descriptions of exemplary programs, research and development efforts, and related information useful in developing effective educational programs.

Through its network of specialized centers or clearinghouses, each of which is responsible for a particular educational area, ERIC acquires, evaluates, abstracts, and indexes current significant information and lists this information in its reference publications.

ERIC/RCS, the ERIC Clearinghouse on Reading and Communication Skills, disseminates educational information related to research, instruction, and professional preparation at all levels and in all institutions. The scope of interest of the Clearinghouse includes relevant research reports, literature reviews, curriculum guides and descriptions, conference papers, project or program reviews, and other print materials related to reading, English, educational journalism, and speech communication.

The ERIC system has already made available—through the ERIC Document Reproduction System—much informative data. However, if the findings of specific educational research are to be intelligible to teachers and applicable to teaching, considerable amounts of data must be reevaluated, focused, and translated into a different context. Rather than resting at the point of making research reports readily accessible, NIE has directed the clearinghouses to work with professional organizations in developing information analysis papers in specific areas within the scope of the clearinghouses.

ERIC is pleased to cooperate with the National Council of Teachers of English in making *The Teacher-Researcher: How to Study Writing in the Classroom* available.

Charles Suhor
Director, ERIC/RCS

Introduction

This book has two purposes, the first immediate and practical and the second long-range and global. The book's practical purpose is as a companion volume to *A Procedure for Writing Assessment and Holistic Scoring* (Myers 1980). It is, like that book, written for teachers who want an introduction to how to conduct school assessments of various kinds, and—to follow up that book—an introduction to what features of writing might be studied after the holistic scoring is complete. The first book described how a group of teachers could select a set of norms (anchor papers) and score a population of papers holistically. Such an activity in a school district develops an awareness that broad agreement on minimum standards is possible and that a follow-up analysis of papers can provide useful information about why some students achieve the minimum standards and some do not.

This book, then, is addressed first to teachers who want some ways to analyze writing samples and the writing process for school or program assessment. The book's second, more global purpose is to promote the development of teacher research among K–12 teachers by providing examples of different ways teachers can study writing in their classrooms. The two purposes are not separate. I regard funds made available for holistic writing assessment and feature analysis as the first serious commitment of a district to teacher research. The norms of a holistic assessment are already present in any interpretive community—a group of potential teacher-researchers, if you will. What needs to be done is to extend this direction into classroom studies funded by a district as part of that district's overall assessment program. I would urge those teachers who plan to use this book as a source of ideas for school assessments to stop a minute and consider the importance of teacher research and the way school assessments can be used to help get funding for teacher research.

The teacher-researcher movement now underway among K–12 teachers is an important part of a professionalization project in which classroom teachers are establishing their special expertise in teaching and curriculum development. In the National Writing Project and some teacher centers, for example, K–12 classroom teachers have become recognized as experts in lesson design, and these teachers have become consultants and leaders of staff development programs and instructors in university programs for teachers. The encouragement of research among teachers is an effort to define an important role for teachers in the development of theory, in the explanation of why some lessons work and others do not.

The teacher-researcher movement among K–12 teachers has been around for at least thirty years. For me, the roots go back to Ben Rust, a social studies teacher in Richmond, California, who in the 1950s and 1960s wrote monographs about how high school students learned world history, how master teachers should function, and how schools are staffed. Another source is Tom Gage, who in 1967, as English Department Head at Concord High School, in Concord, California, organized the first schoolwide holistic writing assessment in the San Francisco Bay Area. He introduced to his department the procedures developed by the Educational Testing Service and ways that teachers might assess the impact of particular curricula. Still another source is a 1975 publication of the New York State English Council entitled *Emphasis: Teachers Doing Research,* with an introduction by Charles Cooper. In 1978, the publications of the National Writing Project began, providing a major force behind the teacher-researcher movement in this country. In the United Kingdom, a major formative influence was Lawrence Sternhouse, who directed in the 1960s a series of teacher-researcher projects for the Schools Council.

All teachers think about what happens in the classroom, but these thoughts are largely undocumented and unreported, and if they are reported they are usually anecdotal and only for lunchroom discussion. In brief, teacher research, because it is unplanned and undocumented, has no institutional standing, and, as a result, few districts provide paid time for teachers to do it; thus education is one of the few professions where expertise in *how* to do its tasks is assigned to people who do not in fact do them. Developing a research tradition among classroom teachers is a way of changing institutional roles and shifting more of the responsibility for teaching expertise to teachers themselves.

This insistence on developing teacher expertise in the design of lessons and in teacher research is not just a matter of professional politics. It is one of the most urgent needs for making schools better places for teaching and learning. Teacher research is one of the ways not only to inspire and renew teacher commitment but also to enable teachers to appreciate the complexity of their own classrooms. Present tests and instruments used in school districts are largely inadequate for diagnosing student needs, and, as a result, this information is almost never used by teachers for guiding instruction. Teacher research can provide a perspective that can guide and inform instruction.

In addition, teachers need some time in an adult environment to discuss ideas and to develop new insights with their colleagues—to learn to be learners again. As it is now, teachers seldom spend time with their colleagues, and when they do the agenda is often set by someone else, and is often focused on administrative or management details, not on lessons or actual student performance. The question is how we can promote and use teacher expertise as a part of the institutional life of the school. The school district workshops of the National Writing Project have shown that staff development sessions run by classroom teachers and focused on the lesson designs of those teachers can become a district's primary resource in curriculum development. But teacher research is still not institutionalized, that is, districts do not use or promote teacher research.

Some people interested in teacher research talk as if teachers should assume research tasks as a professional obligation. These people are often themselves members of institutions of higher education that reward research interests with commendations, promotions, and higher pay. Today, however, K–12 classroom teachers are not promoted, paid, or commended for doing research.

The only exception to this rule is one area—assessment. Under minimum competency statutes, many districts throughout the country have been willing to give teachers the necessary time to score and analyze student writing samples. This institutional setting provides an opportunity to promote funded research by teachers. Just recently I watched a group of San Francisco teachers analyze the data they had collected in their collaborative action research project, otherwise known in the district as the minimum competency assessment. They found, for instance, that the length (total words written) of papers from the bottom to the middle scores showed dramatic gains, but that length in the middle-to-top papers showed only small gains, confirming the intuition of most of the teachers that an emphasis on length and fluency was not equally important for all students.

It is indeed rare in such school assessments for teachers to have the opportunity to design assessment techniques, collect the data, and analyze the results. School assessment methods, like classroom lessons, usually come prepackaged. But holistic assessments, followed by feature analysis, provide a place for teacher research to begin in school districts. As an example of what might be done, two additional steps were needed in the San Francisco situation. First, specific teachers should have been commissioned to write papers describing the results of the feature analysis, and these teachers should have been listed as the authors of the papers. In present practice, someone in the district evaluation office writes the results, and the listed author is the superintendent or his/her deputy. Second, these papers by teachers should be in the district's professional library and should be cited by the district in its official reports. In this way, the district will be encouraging teachers to transcend some of their individual perspectives through the intuitions and findings of their teacher colleagues.

Basic and applied researchers often criticize the kind of research undertaken by the teachers in San Francisco. Some argue that teacher research is simply applied research done badly and that, for example, the San Francisco teachers should not speculate about the trends in their data without submitting those speculations to statistical tests. From the point of view of the basic and applied researcher the significance of any statistical difference—for example, lengths of papers—must be determined by the proper statistical procedures, not by eyeballing the numbers. Yet classroom teachers have usually not been trained in the use of various statistical tests, do not have people available with that expertise, and sometimes do not have the necessary computer capability to handle the numbers.

How does one respond to these criticisms, and others like them, of teacher research? Dixie Goswami, for one, solves the problem by defining teacher research as "naturalistic inquiry procedures which do not result in statistical data toward which journals of education are so heavily biased." In other words, solve the problem of numbers by applying the label "teacher research" only to studies without numbers. This is the solution generally adopted by the teacher-research movement in this country and in the United Kingdom.

Others solve the numbers problem by assigning to the teacher the role of a teacher-partner who works with a basic or applied researcher on a research project (Graves 1981, 111–12):

> The base of research involvement must be broadened to include an active role by the public school teacher. When the teacher becomes involved in research, researchers not only gather better data, but the context of research—the public school classroom—is enriched by the study itself. Teachers and researchers ought to know each other better for the sake of research and the children.

This is what the National Institute of Education and most schools of education mean by teacher research. Obviously, Graves is correct that basic and applied researchers should talk to teachers and form partnerships where appropriate, but I do not consider this a definition of teacher research.

The definition proposed here is the following: *Teacher research is any study conducted by teachers of their school system, school, class, groups of students, or one student, either collaboratively or individually.* But what do we do about the fact that most teachers do not know how to use statistical tests of significance that meet the standards of basic and applied researchers in schools of education? What we do, at least at this time in the historical development of teacher research, is adopt a different standard: *Teacher research will be judged on the basis of its clarity of language, its organizational consistency, and its goodness-of-fit with the intuitions of the teacher community, both in its definitions of problems and in its findings.*

Research by teachers should not be limited to case studies without numbers or partnership roles for teachers, although both can be forms of teacher research. The point of the whole enterprise is to expand the teacher's role as a thinker about learning and teaching. Some of the advantages of counts and numbers in action research are often overlooked by advocates of teacher research who fear that teachers will become "imitative, pseudo-scientific" (Goswami 1984, 349). One of the advantages of numbers is that they allow many teachers to work together on a large project in which they pool data. Many teachers like to begin that way. Another advantage is that in school assessments numbers are often what a district is willing to pay for, providing the necessary funding for promoting teacher inquiry into such things as the writing process.

But the question still remains: How does one respond to the criticisms of basic and applied researchers? They define significance in terms of statistical tests, not an eyeballing of numbers; aim for generalizations about writing on many topics and in many settings, not just the school's selected topics and test settings; and, because they have research responsibilities, have more opportunity to seek optimum solutions to research problems. These three norms of basic and applied researchers— tests of significance, generalizability, and optimizing controls of problems—are defined somewhat differently by classroom teachers engaged in action research. This difference is the same as the fundamental differences Simon (1981) identifies between the science of design and the natural sciences. Teachers, like architects and engineers, are practitioners of a science of design.

The first difference, whether to eyeball numbers or to apply statistical tests, is a question of experience. First, teachers are not taught these tests, and basic and applied researchers are. Perhaps this should change, but, as far as I know, no teacher-preparation program in the country includes introductory statistics as a required course. In any case, the second reason for the difference is even more important. This reason is based on the intuitions that result from experience. Because K–12 classroom teachers see up to ten times as many data each week as do university researchers, these teachers can eyeball numbers to estimate significance and leave the judgment of significance to the intuitions of fellow teachers who read and critique classroom research. That is, K–12 classroom teachers see more students, and from this experience as master teachers develop intuitions about broad patterns and trends among students, just as chess masters develop pattern recognition about chess moves (Simon 1981, 105–7). Thus, when classroom teachers eyeball numbers, they apply their intuition of broad patterns among students as a test of significance. This teacher intuition is, in fact, the primary test of significance in teacher research, and for this reason publishers of teacher research should have it reviewed before publication by a panel of teachers recognized as experts in classroom teaching. Such a test, of course, does not eliminate the use of statistical tests, which can be a means of objectifying and confirming intuitions. This test does, however, raise very important questions about who is a teacher, particularly in grades K through 12. I would argue, for example, that only those who have taught in K–12 classrooms full time for at least seven years should be allowed to list themselves as teachers. The others are assistant and associate teachers, somewhat short of the desired expertise.

The second difference between teacher research and other basic and applied research in schools of education is the degree of generalizability. Teacher research has different goals and, thus, different standards of generalizability. Basic and applied researchers in education have set as their goal the answering of questions about writing on various topics and in various settings both in and out of school. They call this goal "the study of writing as a multiple construct." Teacher-researchers in education, on the other hand, have set as their goal the answering of questions about writing in response to some problem of lesson design in schools (How do students differ in the way they handle an assigned writing task? How does this one student differ from others in the way he or she handles different writing assignments?).

School lessons, like other design problems, usually "imitate appearances in natural things while lacking, in one or many respects, the reality of the latter" (Simon 1981, 8); as a result, although a lesson might attempt to imitate some writing experience in natural events outside of school, the writing experience in the lesson remains a school construct, designed for certain limited goals within the budget and institutional constraints of the school. The lesson often results from interactions among parents, teachers, students, and the school board. Thus, findings from teachers have a dependence on context that cannot be escaped. Yet there are always findings that other teachers can adapt to their own circumstances, and for this reason communities of teacher-researchers are able to develop a body of shared knowledge. In any case, basic and applied researchers should not criticize teacher-researchers for not treating writing as a multiple construct, and teacher-researchers should not criticize basic and applied researchers for not providing lesson designs. The two types of researchers have different goals.

The third difference between the teacher-researcher and the others is that the teacher-researcher has fewer opportunities for optimum solutions to problems. For one thing, the teacher-researcher may know that a question about lesson design requires a particular kind of control or contrasting group, but the classroom teacher as action researcher is limited by circumstances to a particular classroom, school, or district. The teacher-researcher must be encouraged to proceed with what is at hand. For another thing, the classroom teacher may know that natural science says that the reliability of various counts of features in papers can be improved if each feature is counted twice and the two counts averaged, but the budget for the school assessment may not allow such an ideal or optimum solution.

In such a situation, the designer "satisfices," according to Simon, selects a solution, that is, which "suffices" to get the job done and at the same time "satisfies" the need for a solution which, if not the best, is at least better than other alternatives. Says Simon, "No one in his right mind will satisfice if he can equally well optimize; no one will settle for good or better if he can have best. But that is not the way the problem usually poses itself in actual design situations" (Simon 1981, 138). The methods of feature analysis proposed in this book are not always the best, in the sense of satisfying all of the optimum experimental conditions called for in basic and applied research, but they are usually better than some other design alternatives, such as an item analysis of a multiple-choice test on writing skills. Furthermore, in most instances, the methods described have been found to fit comfortably within the surrounding conditions in schools and to have been useful for some teachers attempting to understand learning and teaching in classrooms.

The introduction of teacher research as part of the role of the classroom teacher must lead to changes not only in school districts but also in schools of education. In most schools of education, educational research is conducted for teachers inside K–12 classrooms by people who are outside the K–12 classroom and who may never have worked in a K–12 classroom. Teachers are trained in schools of education as consumers of this educational research, not as future producers of knowledge, and are taught that the experts in K–12 teaching are not K–12 teachers. An introduction to teacher research must become a part of teacher-preparation programs.

This book is intended for teachers who want an introduction to teacher research. Many teachers will read it selectively, examining those sections that seem useful and ignoring those that do not. Probably the best approach is to use the book when one is engaged in a teacher research project. The book has an index so that the reader can return to areas that were not useful on one project but may be useful on another. The next chapter gives a brief review of teacher research procedures, and the chapters that follow give specific examples of various units of analysis—from syntax to social context.

1 Overview of Procedures in Teacher Research

In an article on teacher research, Nancie Atwell (1982) asks, "How can classroom teachers acquire the background in language theory and research procedures to enable them to conduct full, naturalistic investigations of their students' writing processes?" The answer is "By doing it." This book is intended as a handbook for both getting started and keeping going. The way to begin as a teacher-researcher is to keep a research diary in which on-the-spot reflections and questions are recorded. This diary becomes the source of ideas for study. The second way to begin as a teacher-researcher is to establish data-collection routines in the classroom. These routines include using tape recorders to record teacher-student conferences, class discussions, and group work. In addition to using tape recorders, students should maintain portfolios of their writing both in and out of class. In these portfolios, one should find information about students' reading, written work, and out-of-class interests. If these data-collection methods become routine in the classroom, then the methods of a study will not intrude on the rhythm of the class.

The research procedures outlined in this chapter provide some methodological background for beginning classroom research, but not all of these procedures will be possible or even appropriate for them. Furthermore, after a few attempts, other procedures not discussed in this book will begin to become important. What follows are four steps that have been helpful for teacher-researchers organizing a study of writing.

Locating the Problem

Select a problem that is interesting to you and that is found in your classroom, school, or school district. The problem may begin as a learning gap—a student is not doing as well as he or she should—or a learning jump—a student is making remarkable progress. The problem usually begins as a question: "I wonder how this class compares to that one?" or "Why is that student doing so well?" or "What kinds of problems are holding these students back?"

Defining the Problem

Model building in the social sciences requires two kinds of decisions, one theoretical and the other methodological. Defining a problem is a theoretical decision, and selecting a study design, the next section, is a methodological one. The definition of the problem requires that it be placed within some theoretical framework. For example, if one decides to study a student who is struggling to put letters on the page, then one might define the problem as a question of fluency or cognitive processing. Cognitive theory provides several ways of defining the problem—how long are the sentences (T-units) or discourse units (total words) the student writes within a given time period, what kinds of revision does the student make, and what are the stages, if any, in the student's composing process? The essential point here is to select those units of analysis—length, revisions, stages, or whatever—that matter to you or to your fellow teachers. Do not select a unit simply because it is easy to see or count.

It is a mistake to examine a feature without a coherent theory about what the feature represents. Even a bad theory is better than no theory at all because a bad theory will at least produce interpretations that colleagues can criticize and evaluate. Thomas Kuhn makes the point that new theories result from competition among theories and from anomalies or phenomena that cannot be explained by a given theory (1963). Without any theory at all, the teacher-researcher is data-blind, unable to see anything, either sense or nonsense. In the chapters that follow, theories are outlined for the various features suggested for analysis. In reports on school district assessments, these theories can help explain to school boards and others some of the goals of instruction.

Because the theories in these chapters overlap at some points—for example, text theories become cognitive theories about mental representation of texts—a combination of theoretical approaches might be more desirable. This kind of eclecticism is typical of much teacher research where the focus is primarily on learners in context, not the theoretical framework per se. One way to combine different units of analysis is first to conceive of the research as a study of student writing, student attitudes or personality, or teaching techniques. Within student writing, there are product/structure studies or process/procedure studies. A visual matrix or diagram can be a helpful way for a teacher-researcher to shape the theoretical framework underlying the study.

In the product/structure study illustrated in figure 1, the writer has two kinds of choices, one establishing social distance and the other shaping or modeling the form of the discourse. In social distance, the writer uses one of three social forms—conversation (expressive), report (articulation), and argument (conversion). Reports and arguments can be written either as presentations or as rituals, the latter establishing the greatest distance among writer, audience, and subject.

In discourse modeling, the writer can select the form of the personal and expressive, the static (description and classification), or the dynamic (narration and direction). The personal and expressive is a form largely coordinate in its structure, but static and dynamic models can range from coordinate to largely subordinate in structure.

The matrix in figure 1 represents what a teacher might wish to stress in a composition program—a variety of structures or an emphasis on one. The next question is what units in the writing indicate the presence or absence of these different structures. What indicates coordination, subordination, static forms, dynamic forms, arguments, reports, rituals, presentations, and so forth? Examples of these indicators appear in the following chapter. After deciding what indicators to use in the study, the teacher-researcher can use these indicators to locate pieces of writing on the matrix. In figure 1, the various dimensions of the writer's sample will intersect at one point. For example, the writer might produce a static argument written in ritual form with a high degree of subordination. This would place the sample in the upper left-hand corner of the matrix.

A matrix or diagram can also be used to plan process/procedure studies. In figure 2, for example, a writing sample can be located at four different points on the matrix. The vertical line represents time for composing and prewriting, two different points, and the horizontal line represents processing strategies, one point to the left for the size of sentence encoding and one point to the right for the size of discourse encoding. The assumption here is that the weights of time and length will help explain the writing processes of students. Do some students spend no time on prewriting and little time on final drafts? What effect does this have on lengths of discourse and sentences?

One way to diagram the interaction of two variables is the scattergram. In figure 3, for instance, a writing sample that received a grade of 30 points and was preceded by 50 minutes of prewriting becomes data point A on the scattergram. The patterns of the data points suggest the relationship between the two variables. In figure 3, there appears to be no systematic relationship. In figure 4, grade points increase as prewriting time increases, suggesting that prewriting may contribute to an improvement in the quality of the writing, while in figure 5, grade points go down as prewriting increases, suggesting that the prewriting these students do may contribute to a decrease in the quality of the writing. What needs to be examined is whether the prewriting or the grading differs between the two classes.

I. *Structures*

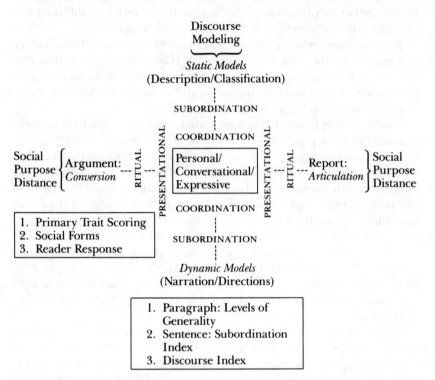

Figure 1. Theoretical framework for a product/structure study.

II. *Procedures*   *Prewriting (or Draft 1)*

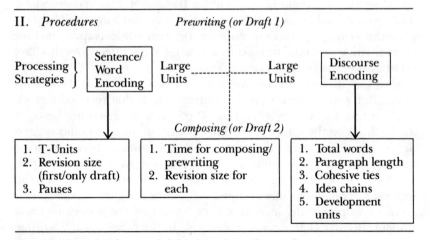

Figure 2. Theoretical framework for a process/procedure study.

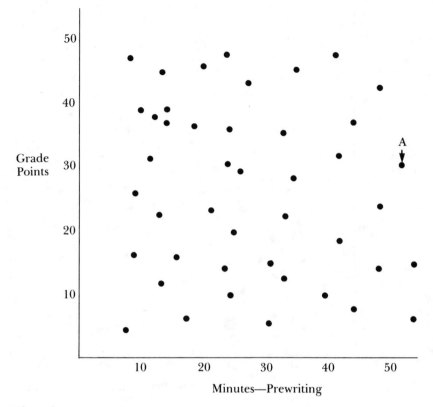

Figure 3

Later chapters will present examples of other diagrams that teacher-researchers can use to shape the theoretical outlines of their studies and to examine results. Chapter 5, for example, has a matrix showing the interaction of teaching practices and the personality needs of students. This matrix guided the study of Ada Hill and Beth Boone, teacher-researchers from Virginia (Hill and Boone 1982). It is important to remember that a theory is only a way of sorting out possible answers. It is not necessarily *the* answer. So, too, a correlation is not a cause. Simply that students with high SAT scores have more bathrooms at home does not mean that more bathrooms produce higher SAT scores. However, more bathrooms may have an association with something that is a possible cause. For instance, more bathrooms may be associated with families who have the money to hire SAT tutors for their children. The rule: when it comes to causal relationships, use *might be*, not *is*.

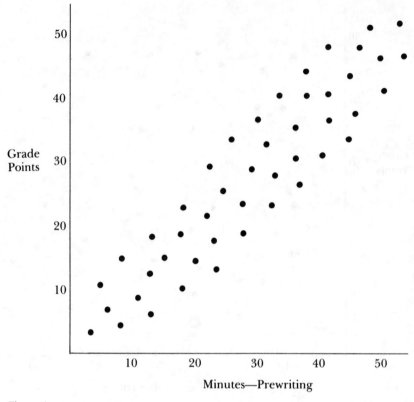

Figure 4

Selecting an Overall Design

Design is the methodological approach to problem definition, and in a sense problem definition and design cannot be separated. At least three overall designs are available: rationalism, positivism, and contextualism. Each of these designs takes a different approach to the key concerns of significance, reliability, and validity. Significance is a question of importance—Is the result a matter of chance or does the result matter to anybody?—and reliability refers to the likelihood of obtaining the same answer if one were to measure the same thing twice. Validity has two aspects and requires that the identified variables in a research project be variables existing in actual human events. Internal validity requires that the data come from an authentic setting, and external validity requires that the findings be generalizable to other groups in similar settings.

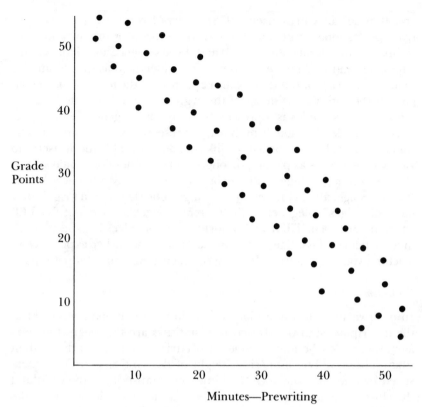

Figure 5

Rationalism

In a rationalist design, the teacher-researcher examines contrasting pieces of data and uses the logic of reason and the insight of intuition to make claims about the significance, reliability, and validity of a hypothesis. One key feature of rationalist research is that the findings are not embedded in a particular context. For example, Chomsky examined two contrasting sentences ("John is easy to please" and "John is eager to please") and hypothesized the existence of a deep structure in which the two sentences had different subjects ("Somebody pleases John" and "John pleases somebody"). Chomsky attempted to describe a model of innate competence by describing the contrasting surface data of performance (Chomsky 1965).

In another example, Cicero, in *De Oratore*, contrasted the parts of written texts and found the existence of such forms as *exordium* (introduction) and *perporatio* (summing up). Likewise, Francis Christensen

and Bonniejean Christensen (1978) analyzed contrasting paragraphs
from professional writers and found three forms of organization (coordinate, subordinate, and mixed) and three sentence additions (nouns,
adjectives, and -ed/-ing verbs) in what they identified as the cumulative
sentence. In each of these rationalist approaches the test of an idea's validity is the logical consistency of the argument and the reader's recognition of the examples as representative of his or her general experience.

An example of rationalism in teacher research is an examination by
Gail Siegel et al. of sequences of instruction, K–13: "I find it useful to
view young writers as passing through a series of developmental stages:
(1) Transcribing Stage, (2) Re-copying Stage, (3) Sentences/Whole
Phrases Stage, and (4) Independent Stage. The stages aren't rigid; they
have soft edges" (Siegel et al. 1980, 1). Ms. Siegel, a teacher at Reed Elementary School in Tiburon, California, does not place her speculations
in a particular class. She talks in general about what her experience in
teaching young children tells her about their developmental patterns.

Positivism

In positivism the test of an idea's reliability is the numerical weight of
the descriptive statistics. Descriptive statistics are the mean (the average), the mode (the most frequently occurring point), and the median
(the midpoint). The numerical weight of descriptive statistics is measured by inference statistics. The inference statistics are the t-test and
the chi-square, among others, and they can tell us to what degree the
numerical results are a matter of chance. What is chance? Among other
things, chance can be the amount of error which can result when one
averages scores with a great range and diversity, or the limits of estimation when the sample size is small.

Most writing researchers are willing to accept a 5 percent risk of
chance results. That is, if the probability of chance results can be reduced to one out of twenty, then the writing researcher will accept the
result as statistically significant. The probability of exceeding 5 percent
risk of error can, of course, be reduced by increasing the number of
data. If the number is big enough, the result will represent the world as
it is, not chance based on a limited sample.

If you are using score averages to compare groups, ask your school
research department to help you apply a test of significance to the differences. If you want to try a statistical test, then see the section on statistics in appendix C. It is important to remember that a result may be
statistically significant, not a matter of statistical chance, and at the same
time not be experimentally significant. Experimental significance requires that the subjects in a writing experiment be randomly assigned

to different experimental treatments, matching the subjects and the situation on all the variables except the key one for the experiment. These experimental controls are very difficult, if not impossible, for most teacher-researchers, working as they do in actual schools and classrooms, and teacher-researchers who use matching-group designs should simply acknowledge the difficulties and indicate the areas where matching may not have occurred. A typical matching design that controls for the fact that topics may not be perfectly matched in pre–post comparisons is shown in figure 6.

Appendix B is a section on evaluation designs by Eash, Talmage, and Walberg. Teachers who wish to use a positivist approach to evaluation will find in this section an outline of four possible designs: (1) a true experimental design in a field setting, (2) a nonequivalent control group design, (3) a time series design, and (4) a no-comparison-group design.

One of the major problems in positivism is validity. The reason for this is that most studies have to exchange validity for reliability or vice versa. In positivism, the emphasis on reliability, using high standards for controlling and numbering data, leads to a loss of validity. The data are reliable, but they look less and less like actual classroom experience. In the design below, the effort to get two matching topics may lead to a topic that is not typical of classroom experience, and the split in the class

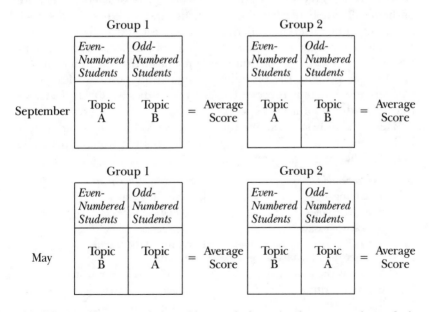

Figure 6. Matching-group design with controls for topics that may not be perfectly matched.

between topic A and topic B may reduce the between-student exchanges of information and assistance typical of classroom writing.

In writing research, the studies of Bateman and Zidonis (1966) and Mellon (1969) are examples of positivism, both using control and experimental groups to test the hypothesis that instruction in grammar or sentence combining increases what Mellon calls "syntactic maturity" and what Bateman and Zidonis call "structural complexity." Frank O'Hare (1973), also using control and experimental groups, examined not only whether sentence-combining instruction of his design would increase syntactic maturity but whether teachers would give higher ratings to those papers with syntactic maturity.

For teacher-researchers, the positivist design has serious limitations. Teachers have not been trained in statistics and experimental design and their attempts at a positivist design are certain to fall below the standards set by basic and applied researchers. Even so, I am suggesting that teachers attempt such studies if they desire to do so and that teacher-researchers adopt, at least for the present, a different standard of estimation. Teacher-researchers should be allowed in their studies to eyeball numbers, depending on the intuition of readers for judgments of the overall acceptability of the results. In other words, for teacher-researchers, positivist studies will be largely interpretive, not strictly empirical. In time, as the professionalization of teachers increases, more and more of them will have better training in statistics and experimental design— a training quite different from that given to basic and applied researchers—and at some later date the community of teacher-researchers may wish to adopt more rigorous standards for positivist research by teachers. For the present, the prevailing standard for positivist designs by teacher-researchers is represented by such studies as Robert Tierney's (see appendix D for a full report).

Tierney's study is an examination of two ways of teaching high school biology, one in an experimental group with many writing experiences and the other in a control group with little or no writing (1981, 52):

Experimental Group	*Control Group*
1. reading logs	1. no reading logs
2. neuron notes	2. no neuron notes
3. practice essays	3. no practice essays
4. writing to a specific audience other than the teacher	4. writing to the teacher as an examiner
5. end-of-class summaries	5. no end-of-class summary
6. group writing	6. limited group writing
7. essay tests	7. multiple-choice tests

During the first semester, Tierney, a biology teacher at Irvington High School in Fremont, California, taught the experimental group, and another teacher taught the control group. During the second semester, Tierney taught the control group, and the other teacher taught the experimental group. Tierney found that although the pre–posttest differences between the two groups were mixed, the experimental group consistently did better on the recall tests, which were given sixteen weeks after the first unit and three weeks after the second.

Tierney examines students in two classes, but sometimes teacher-researchers want to examine a sample of students from many schools and at the same time claim that the sample represents the population in the schools. In order to select a sample representing the population, one must use random sampling methods. These methods ensure that every possible sample of a particular size has an equal chance of being selected from the population. A group of volunteers, for example, is not random or representative of the total population because volunteers may only include those students who want to please the teacher and get the best grades.

One commonly used random sampling procedure is to number the students in the population, using the roll book numbers in the class plus a different number for each class; turn to the table in Appendix C, close your eyes, and put your finger on the page, the beginning digits in the first number you touch being the first student in the sample; and then move three numbers left or right, up or down, for the next student, continuing this procedure until you have your sample.

Contextualism

Contextualism is the third methodological choice. Although positivism has been the dominant method of research in writing, an increasing number of researchers has started to criticize the positivist assumption that in the pursuit of general laws in the social sciences one must strip away context and put subjects in an experimental or laboratory setting.

Contextualism differs from positivism in that it examines subjects in their natural settings without imposing any experimental constraints from the outside. For example, Graves (1975) began his study by examining the writing folders of ninety-four students in four classrooms, finally arriving at a tentative three-phase structure for the writing process (prewriting, composing, and postwriting). Next he observed fifty-three writing episodes in four classrooms, and finally he gathered data on one student, including interviews with parents. Contextualism differs from rationalism in that contextualism examines writing as an evolutionary process, collecting data over extended periods of time in a "natural" context, whereas rationalism examines writing as a product, collecting examples of the end result.

Wallace Chafe's work is an example of contextualism, and Northrop Frye's is an example of rationalism. Chafe (1980) examined story structure by showing subjects in a six-minute film about a boy who steals a basket of pears from a man and then asking subjects to tell "what happened in the film." Chafe focused on how stories evolve in a given context. Frye (1957), on the other hand, collected what he considered a representative number of completed stories and then described the categories into which the stories might fall (romantic, ironic, and so forth). The difference is the same one that David Olson believes separates Chafe and Chomsky. Olson (1977) says that Chomsky believes that language is best represented by the written text, and Chafe believes that language is best represented by oral conversational utterances.

Contextual studies can be clinical or episodic. The clinical approach, used by Jean Piaget and Barbel Inhelder in their study of a child's concept of conservation, requires the researcher to give the student the writing problem. Chafe's study, described above, and Janet Emig's (1971) are other examples. Emig asked eight students, selected by teachers, to write about a person or event. She then asked these students to discuss what writing they liked to do, how they usually went about their writing tasks, and what writing conditions in school were like.

The episodic study is one like Claudia Mitchell-Kernan's 1972 study of black discourse in Oakland, California. She recorded conversations heard in her neighborhood and selected particular episodes for study, for example, the situation in which a speaker "puts down" another person. Other examples are William Labov's 1972 study of oral narratives told on Harlem street corners and his 1977 study with David Fanshell of the discourse used in therapy.

Sometimes episodic studies try to show the kind of language used during a particular part of the school day. Jenny Cook-Gumperz, John Gumperz, and Herbert Simons (1979) have described procedures that natural science researchers often use in order to do an episodic study of language in a school setting:

1. Selection of fieldwork site: The people who work at the site must be willing to be evaluators of data.

2. Observing the organization of the school day: Because the study of language in school settings describes events over time, the time framework must be segmented in some way. The segmentation might be the school bell schedule.

3. Identifying activity grouping: Observations of the class and interviews with teachers will help the observer to group activities. An example would be art time (drawing pictures) and storytelling (or show and tell).

4. Selection of key episodes: These episodes will be those that seem to reveal something interesting about the writing process. For instance, one might select all incidents of miscommunication, the teacher's method of assigning writing, or the kinds of stories children develop in their prewriting and art.

At other times, episodic studies try to show how language varies from one writing assignment to another. These are assignments selected by the teacher, not the researcher. At still other times, the episodic study examines writing in general in the classroom, no matter what the assignment. An example of this kind of episodic study is Kellogg Hunt's study (1965) of how many clauses children at different ages could consolidate into a single sentence. Hunt collected one thousand words from each student. Each writing episode was part of the normal coursework and free of any control from Hunt. His findings showed, for instance, that the average eighth grader could consolidate five clauses, the average fourth grader only three.

Another example of an episodic study is Anne Haas Dyson and Celia Genishi's examination of cooperative exchanges between students writing in the elementary classroom. Their approach is to present the data and then to offer some possible generalizations about them (1982, 129):

> Tambrea appeared to feel a responsibility or a desire to teach, to share her writing ability with her peers. For example, in the following interaction, Peter begins by asking Eva for help, but Tambrea quickly intervenes:
>
> Peter: How do you spell *have*? (Peter directs the question to Eva.)
> Tambrea: I think I know.
> Peter: You do?
> Tambrea: I think. I think. Anyway, whatta ya tryin' to write?
> Peter: I'm writing about my picture. (Peter shows his photo to Tambrea.)
> Tambrea: I know, but whatta ya tryin' to write?
> Peter: Right here, my picture. (Peter sounds irritated.)
> Tambrea: Whatta ya tryin' to write, anyway?
> Peter: "I have a picture of a cat in my house."
> Tambrea: What do you want to write? (Tambrea now sounds irritated.)
> Peter: I want to make "I have (unclear)." (Peter points to a word on his paper.)
> Tambrea: Um kay. Just put an *S* (sic) and then. . . .

> Peter finally realized that Tambrea was using *write* as a synonym for
> *spell* and showed her what word he needed to know.
>   While Tambrea composed the following story, she offered un-
> solicited advice twice, but other children's appeals interrupted her
> four times.

An example of a clinical contextual study in teacher research is Ada
Hill and Beth Boone's 1982 study of the relationship of Abraham Maslow's personality theory to writing. The scales that they gave students
were not natural parts of a writing class, but were presented in the class
setting as a way of estimating personality development, very much the
way Piaget presented children with a task in order to estimate their in-
tellectual development. The scales did, however, use tasks from the classroom setting as a basis for estimating personality development.

The episodic contextual study is represented by the studies of Nancy
Marashio, a teacher of eighth graders at Center School in Windham,
New Hampshire, and Jerry Herman, a teacher at Laney Community
College in Oakland, California. The difference between the two is that
Jerry Herman is studying a single case, and Nancy Marashio is studying
116 eighth graders. Herman (1979) is describing the work and reactions
of a single student at various points in the student's visits to the college
tutorial center. Marashio (1982) is describing the responses of students
in different classes in a particular school to the panic of a first writing
assignment, their strategies for giving their writing structure, and their
evaluations of their own writing. Marashio presents examples and illustrations of what she believes are general patterns, but she does not attempt to crunch numbers into averages and percentages, as does
Tierney. The "Try Scale" of student Pete Bolin is one example Marashio
presents—in this case, an example of a student's strategy for controlling
his own writing processes (1982, 61):

> I base my writing on a scale. I call this scale my try scale. I base
> my try scale on these tries.
>   1. I try to write on the subject given every week.
>   2. I try to put my ideas together.
>   3. I try to write things that interest me while staying in the
>   boundaries of the subject given.
>   4. I try to make my themes a little funny.
>   5. I try to make a 4 theme, but that isn't always so.
>   6. I try to use my try scale.
>   I made this scale to model the way I write themes. Those tries are
> how I model myself. I use this try scale most of the time.

Limitations and Future Questions

Try listing during the study the things the study did not try to do and
the modifications you would make if you did the study again as ideas oc-

cur to you. For example, one problem in many cross-sectional studies (a comparison of third graders and tenth graders on a given writing assignment, for instance) is that they are not, strictly speaking, studies of chronological development. Yet school districts like to compare different grade levels and then to claim that grade-level differences are developmental. Some teacher-researcher somewhere should convince a district that it should assess a single group of students over a long period of time. A notable example of such a study is Walter Loban's study of 211 students from kindergarten through the twelfth grade in the Oakland Unified School District, Oakland, California.

It is helpful for other teacher-researchers if the list of limitations is translated into other kinds of research questions which they can pursue in their classrooms. When teachers analyze papers in the school district assessment, their final comment is often "Next year let's look at. . . ."

Most school district assessments involve teams of teacher-researchers, but most school site studies involve only one or two teachers. Furthermore, nine out of ten studies by teacher-researchers are case studies of one or two students. Donald Graves has made a suggestion that depth needs to be added to school site studies, using case, ethnographic (or contextual and episodic), and experimental (positivist) approaches within the *same* study. This kind of study, outlined by Graves (1981, 110–11) below, will require a team effort and could provide the framework for a useful department or grade-level project:

> Depth needs to be added through different use of case, experimental, and ethnographic procedures *within the same study*. In short, the space-time dimensions of research must be expanded to include procedures in the same study that in the past have been used solely for one type of study alone. An example of such a study focusing on children is contained in Figure 13.

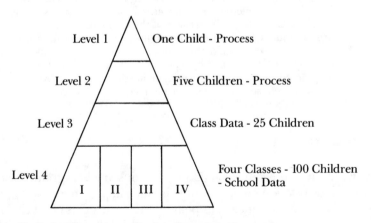

Figure 13. Design illustrating space-time dimensions of research.

In such a design, data are gathered simultaneously at four levels of investigation: intensive process data through direct observation of the child at Levels 1 and 2 over at least one year's time, and the full context of writing episodes are gathered from before the child writes until the child has had a response to the product. The child in Level 1 is a writer who gives more than the usual amount of information, involves a broader spectrum of development, and therefore merits more time from the researcher. Level 3 data come from the entire class in which Level 1 and 2 children reside. Some informal observations are taken from them but all of their products are classified or duplicated for examination. Finally, product analysis is applied to four classes within the same school building, including each of the first three levels of the study. In this way, product analyses of larger groups can be further investigated for their process implications in the case study data. Similarly, case data variables that appear to be pivotal can be examined through interventions or product analyses at Levels 3 and 4. To date, three studies have been done in this manner: Graves (1973)(1979–80) and Calkins (1980).

Depth must be added through more intensive case studies with intra-differences (within the child differences) explained through one case. One child's behavior is described within the context of at least one to three years. In this way, the pattern of development within one variable or across variables can be examined and explained over a much longer period of time. Too often research contributes to a lottery philosophy of educating. That is, we look for similarities across children, ways of generalizing one child's behavior to aid other children. There is a value in this, but there is also a grave, potential weakness. We will look too quickly to see why the child before us is *the same* as other children rather than look at how the child is different. Or, if the difference is located, we seek to extinguish it in order to integrate the child into a homogeneous mass for more convenient instruction.

In short, we tend to overlook the one thing that makes the child different, unique. We tend to overlook the voice—the one experience or knowledge area the child knows well. Good teachers have responded to this uniqueness on an intuitive basis for years. Research needs to document intra-differences of the components that make children unique. Glenda Bissex (1980), in her study of Paul over a five-year period, conducted this type of study. Also, the child in Level 1 (Figure 13) is a potential type for study of intra-differences. Data gathered in such depth usually point the way to discovering new variables not seen in the larger data gathering. We cannot afford to be without such studies.

The Write-Up

The write-up of the study should begin with some background about why the issue or question of the study became important to you in your classroom. It is important at this point to cite the insights of other class-

room teachers whose previous work, whether in the form of teacher research, lunchroom conversation, or ditto sheets, has been helpful. This
beginning step, if it becomes a convention in teacher research, will help
to establish in writing the network of a professional community of teachers and to provide for classroom teachers a history of their ideas. That
history has largely been lost because teachers have not recognized their
professional roles as writers and experts in lesson design.

In addition, the write-up should explicitly describe the design of the
study, and enough data should be made available so that the reader can
make some kind of independent judgment of the results. If possible, always attach samples of student work.

Chapter Summary

1. Start a research diary.
2. Establish data-collection routines in the classroom such as portfolios and tapes.
3. Locate the problem in general experience, a school district, a
   school, a class, a student, or a group of students.
4. Define the problem within a theoretical framework (e.g., syntax,
   text, information processing, social context, personal psychology)
   and use diagrams, where helpful, to map interactions.
5. Select a research design:
   - a. Rationalism: (1) Select paradigm or norm.
     (2) Identify data suggesting norm or paradigm.
   - b. Positivism: (1) Define unit to be studied.
     (2) Identify a treatment (lesson variable) that might have an interesting influence on unit to be studied.
     (3) Match groups and other variables so that one can see the variation in the unit to be studied when the treatment is applied.
   - c. Contextualism: (1) Identify unit to be studied.
     (2) Identify context of the unit, either the normal episodes that have the unit or the clinical test that will elicit the unit if the test is inserted into the normal context.
6. Do the study.
7. Present the background of the study, the data, and an interpretation of the results.
8. Identify the limitations and unanswered questions in the study.

2 Syntax

Each of the next four chapters introduces various theoretical frameworks within which researchers have been working. Each chapter discusses a different level of analysis—syntax, text, information processing, and social context. The final chapter focuses on errors, teaching practices, and student attitudes toward writing. Within these levels, different features are identified, and the theory surrounding each feature is briefly described. The place to begin for teacher-researchers is *replication*. If you find a feature and theory of interest, replicate in your classroom the study of another researcher. This is a way not only to contribute to our knowledge about English education but also to learn how research is done. The chapter that follows examines features within two theories of syntax—transformational grammar and case grammar.

1 Feature: Syntactic Maturity or Fluency

Theory: Transformational Grammar

Chomsky argues that there is a single ideal of language competence, based on "an ideal speaker-listener in a completely homogeneous speech community" (1965, 3), and that this ideal reflects universals of all language and fundamental operations of the human mind. It is at the level of syntax, he says, that the language reveals most clearly that it is rule-governed and not arbitrary. He suggests two sets of rules as primary: phrase structure rules for inserting words from a mental dictionary into sentence slots in deep structure, and transformation rules for adding, deleting, and moving material around in deep-structure sentences and thereby producing surface structure. In this way, two deep-structure sentences such as "The man is winning" and "You know the man" can become the single sentence "Is the man whom you know winning?"

Chomsky argued that structural linguistics, the grammar that preceded transformational grammar, did not account for the differences between such sentences as "John is easy to please" and "John is eager to please" because structural grammar analyzed only the common surface structure of the two sentences—noun-verb-adjective-infinitive—not the deep structure where transformations had taken place. In the deep structure of the first sentence, someone who does not appear on the surface is trying to please John ("John is easy to please"), but in the deep structure of the other sentence, John is the subject eager to please someone who does not appear on the surface ("John is eager to please").

What Chomsky did for the teaching of composition was shift attention from the surface structure to the history or processes which produced the sentence. Some of these processes, particularly transformations that consolidate and embed clauses, are reflected in the length of Kellogg Hunt's T-unit, which is a main clause and all of its modifiers. Hunt (1965), examining what he called "syntactic maturity" in the writing of adults in *Harper's* and *Atlantic* magazines and of fifty-four students in grades four, eight, and twelve, found that adults have longer T-units (more words per T-unit) and a larger ratio of clauses to T-units, a measure of subordination.

Hunt's study raised the question of whether or not special lessons in different sentence transformations might not accelerate the growth of syntactic maturity in students. John Mellon (1969), labeling this growth "syntactic fluency" instead of "syntactic maturity," found that sentence combining practice did indeed lead to growth, but he also found that students who improved their syntactic fluency did not necessarily receive higher essay scores than students who had not improved. Frank O'Hare (1973), on the other hand, modifying Mellon's exercises slightly, found that both essay scores and syntactic fluency improved as a result of direct instruction in sentence combining. These studies and others have over the past ten years helped give direction to an increasing number of teaching approaches emphasizing sentence combining.

Lesson: Sentence Combining

Lessons in sentence combining are not the same as most lessons with direct instruction in conventional or transformational grammar. Mellon's study, for instance, specifically says, "The growth produced by the sentence combining treatment represents a significant enhancement of normal growth, regardless of whether the latter is defined in a curriculum environment featuring conventional grammar, or in one with no grammar study of any kind" (Mellon 1969, 62). In any event, most schools that teach sentence combining consider such lessons part of the grammar program, and typically sentence combining is used for ten or fifteen minutes each day, each lesson presenting a particular problem and each problem somewhat harder than the previous one.

There is some debate about what sentence combining actually teaches. Mellon, for instance, observes, "In a word, the differences between mature and immature writing are a result more of elaboration than of condensation" (Mellon 1969, 58). In other words, students are not combining what they would formerly have written separately; they are elaborating more on what they are writing. The students may have a tacit knowledge of various linguistic operations but not exercise it. In such a view what is being taught and learned in sentence combining is surface structure combination, not transformations of deep structure. Sentence-combining lessons tend to vary in their cuing systems. Some early materials follow closely the models used by Mellon (Brown and White 1968). Other materials use O'Hare's modification of Mellon's cuing system, changing six of Mellon's grammatical terms to the actual morphemes used to make a given transformation. For instance, *T-infinitive* in Mellon becomes in O'Hare *FOR + TO*. William Strong made a major contribution to teachers when he dropped the cuing system altogether and put the sentences in the context of larger pieces (Strong 1973).

Topic and Test Conditions

Teacher-researchers should remember that the subject matter of, and preparation time allowed for, writing assignments can have an important effect on the syntactic features of the writing produced. On the issue of subject matter, Hunt found that "fourth graders wrote stories that told what people said; the twelfth graders wrote about what Pope believed and Huxley believed about the state of mankind. Fourth graders don't ordinarily write on such subjects. . . . The shift in noun clauses is linked to maturity by being linked to subject matter" (1965, 151). Mellon has made a similar argument, suggesting that because their perceptions of the world become elaborated in different ways as students grow older, changes in structure may primarily reflect changes in subject matter (1969).

On the issue of testing time, Eleanor Keenan found substantial differences between the syntax of planned and that of unplanned discourse. In unplanned discourse, which does not require planning time, she found fewer subordinators such as *if* and *because* (Keenan 1978), suggesting that extra planning time may contribute to more frequent use of subordinators. If syntactic features are to be counted in an assessment, then the topic and planning time must be carefully considered. The problem for the assessment designer is that although more "academic" topics may generate more heavily embedded sentences in the writing of some students, such topics may not reflect the topics used in typical lessons or the topics designated as important by community committees and boards deciding school goals.

Coding of Features and Patterns of Use

The features listed below are some of those that have been used to estimate how much students consolidate and embed their clauses:

Length of T-Unit

The T-unit is a main clause and all of its modifiers. All of the following are T-units (from Hunt 1965, 21):

  a. I like the movie we saw about Moby Dick, the white whale.
  b. The captain said if you can kill the white whale, Moby Dick, I will give the gold to the one that can do it.
  c. And it is worth sixteen dollars.
  d. They tried and tried.

Mellon used the following decision rules for his T-unit counts, following essentially the same procedure used by Hunt (Mellon 1969, 43):

  1. Each independent clause, including all constituent constructions, counts as one T-unit.
  2. Clauses of condition, concession, reason, and purpose (although traditionally considered constituents of independent clauses) also count as separate T-units.
  3. Independent clauses occurring as directly quoted discourses count as T-units. Speaker tags are discarded.
  4. Orthographic sentence fragments count as part of the T-unit to which they belong.
  5. True fragments resulting from the omission of a single word count as T-units with the missing word supplied. Other true fragments are discarded.
  6. Unintelligible word strings, vocatives, interjections, and various parenthetical or a-syntactic expressions found in conversational writing are discarded.
  7. Independent clauses differing from preceding clauses only in their subject, and thus elliptical beyond their verb auxiliary, are discarded.

The steps to determine the average number of words per T-unit are: (1) count the total words in the sample, (2) count the number of T-units in the sample, and (3) divide the number of words by the number of T-units.

$$\text{Average number of words per T-unit} = \frac{\text{Number of words in sample}}{\text{Number of T-units in sample}}$$

Teacher-researchers who do frequency studies must keep a record of the decision rules that govern counts and the reasons for the rules.

Counting in language studies is always harder than it seems at first. Mellon counted compound nouns written solid as one word, and counted as two words compound nouns written separately and hyphenated word pairs. He also counted as one word phrasal proper names (e.g., the Bronx Bomber), dates, and aphorisms from composition topics.

Hunt reports the following patterns of T-unit length (average number of words in a T-unit): 8.6 in grade 4, 11.5 in grade 8, and 13 in grade 12 (Hunt 1965, 22). Rubin and Piche (1979, 303) report 8.86 (grade 4), 11.59 (grade 8), and 14.15 (grade 12). Crowhurst (1980, 225) reports the following variation of T-unit length by grade level and mode:

Grade 6	Narration	10.60	Argument	13.79
Grade 10	Narration	12.48	Argument	15.17
Grade 12	Narration	12.51	Argument	16.06

Loban (1976, 27) reports the following number of words per communication unit (same as T-unit) for high, random, and low groups:

	High	Random	Low
Grade 3:	7.68	7.60	5.65
Grade 4:	8.83	8.02	6.01
Grade 5:	9.52	8.76	6.29
Grade 6:	10.23	9.04	6.91
Grade 7:	10.83	8.94	7.52
Grade 8:	11.24	10.37	9.49
Grade 9:	11.09	10.05	8.78
Grade 10:	12.59	11.79	11.03
Grade 11:	11.82	10.69	11.21
Grade 12:	14.06	13.27	11.24

Loban (1976, 25–26) comments,

> A high average number of words per communication unit could simply be the result of verbosity—an increased use of language without any significant increase in meaningful communication. In this research, however, this has not proved to be the case. Almost without exception, a high average number of words per unit is accompanied by a high teacher's rating on language skill, by a more effective use of phrases and clauses, and by the increased use of other forms of elaboration contributing to clear and meaningful communication. For this reason, the average number of words per communication unit has proved to be one of the most crucial measures of fluency developed during the course of this investigation.

Ratio of Clauses to T-units

Length of T-unit indicates some things about the complexity of student writing at the sentence level, but it does not indicate whether that complexity involves an increased use of subordination. As one indicator of subordination at the sentence level, Hunt suggests the ratio of clauses to T-units: "Not only is the ratio of clauses to T-units a convenient arithmetical bridge, but it also provides by direct inspection an indication of how frequently a subordinate clause was added to a main clause" (Hunt 1965, 35). This ratio indicates subordination through clause-embedding transformations by dividing the number of all clauses by the number of main clauses or T-units.

$$\text{Ratio of clauses to T-units} = \frac{\text{All clauses (subordinate + main clauses)}}{\text{Main clauses}}$$

Hunt reports the following patterns of the ratio of clauses to T-units: averages were 1.30 in grade 4, 1.42 in grade 8, and 1.68 in grade 12 (Hunt 1965, 35). Rubin and Piche (1979, 303) report 1.58 for grade 4, 1.51 for grade 8, 1.64 for grade 12, and 1.61 for adults. Teacher-researchers can use these findings as an indicator either of group deviation from the norm reported by other researchers or of problems in the design of the study, leading to skewed results.

Noun and Adjective Embedding

On the theoretical grounds that different embeddings require different skills, different types of consolidations and embeddings can also be counted. Hunt counted the different types of words used to introduce various types of clauses: nouns (that, how, why), adverbs (if, while, until), and adjectives (who, whom, which). He found "no statistically significant increase in adverbial clauses, from grade to grade, though the increase in noun clauses and adjective clauses is statistically significant" (Hunt 1965, 80)

$$\text{Noun and adjective embedding index} = \frac{\text{Subordinators for noun clauses (that, how, why) or adjective clauses (who, which, that)}}{\text{Total words}}$$

Hunt (1965), Loban (1976), and others have used different ways of reporting the use of different clauses. Therefore, there is no general standard that can be reported. Mellon reports some interesting ideas, however, on the use of nominalism as an indicator of conceptual development in student writing. He was interested in trying to distinguish between conceptual networking and syntactic manipulations. In his study, Mellon counts as nominal clauses the factive and interrogative clauses occurring in nominal positions, including appositive clauses ("The fact that it rained amused him"), and the WH + ever clauses ("He did whatever she asked"). Mellon did not count adjective complements ("He was glad that she was sad") and fact-like comparative clauses ("It was so cold that his feet froze") as nominals on the grounds that these noun clauses were not naming concepts in the same way that factive and interrogative clauses were.

The total number of clauses counted was then divided by total T-units. Mellon's experimental group, which practiced sentence-combining problems, showed an increase of 14.35 to 17.76 (index multiplied by 100), whereas the control group, which did exercises in traditional grammar and usage texts, showed a drop in nominal-clause usage (Mellon 1969, 52).

Mellon also counted noun phrases. A verbal, in order to count as a noun phrase, had to retain at least one constituent "from its deep structure" (Mellon 1969, 46). "The man's arrival" and "the settlement of the case" counted, but "the arrival" and "the settlement" did not. Neither did adjective complements ("He was anxious to please her"), infinitival predicate complements ("He forced her to leave"), and catenated verb phrases ("He tried to fry the rice"). "He tried frying the rice" did count, as did other gerund, infinitive, and derived-noun phrases occurring in nominal positions ("He left without saying a word").

These nominal phrases were counted and then divided by the total number of T-units. Mellon's experimental group showed an increase in the nominal phrase index from 5.86 to 9.74 (index multiplied by 100), and the control group showed a drop (Mellon 1969, 52). Mellon concluded in a later review, "Only the increase of restrictive embeddedness in dominant NP's deserves to be labeled growth" (Mellon 1979, 28). His point is that it is the child's growing network of conceptual knowledge that is responsible for the greater complexity of nouns and their restrictive modifiers, not sentence combining. Sentence combining provides assistance in putting together the growing network of concepts, but, according to Mellon, does not itself generate the greater complexity of ideas. In other words, Mellon is claiming that sentence combining is effective only if combined with wide reading and/or exploration of ideas.

One approach to indexing the dominant NP is to count the average number of words in subject phrases, counting the subject words themselves, only the subject modifiers before the subject, and only the restrictive modifiers after the subject. The long string of prepositional phrases after the subject may present a conceptual difficulty. Are those phrases conceptual networking or loose associations? The general rule is to count only the first prepositional phrase after the subject, all words in restrictive adjective clauses (who, which, that), all words in restrictive infinitive phrases after the subject, and all words in restrictive participial phrases, both past and present.

$$\text{\begin{tabular}{c} Dominant NP \\ conceptual index \\ (words per \\ subject NP) \end{tabular}} = \frac{\text{Modifers + subject nominal + restrictive modifiers}}{\text{Total subject nominals}}$$

The following sentences are an example of such a count:

1. *The man who owns the car* is here. = 6
2. *My friend,* who owns the car, is here. = 2
3. *The captain,* holding the wheel in his hand, died. = 2
4. *The man's arrival from the South Seas* was unexpected. = 7

The theoretical foundation for counts of dominant NPs is uncertain at best. As Mellon has indicated, "Research on growth of restrictive dominant NP structure is needed" (Mellon 1979, 28). At this point, counting the number of words in NPs in the subject position appears to be one way of indexing the fact that mature writers see and say much more in fewer sentences and, to paraphrase Mellon, are required by their maturing conceptual knowledge to make additional restrictive, secondary statements in each independent clause (Mellon 1979, 18).

2 Feature: Clear and Direct Sentences

Theory: Case Grammar and Stylistics

One of the principles of early transformational grammar was that if two surface structures derive from exactly the same deep structure and if their derivations differ only in the fact that an optional transformation has been applied to one and not the other, then the two surface structures must have the same meaning (Katz and Postal 1964). By this meaning-preserving principle, the two sentences "Many people read few books" and "Few books are read by many people" must mean the same thing because the only difference between the two sentences is the optional passive transformation in the last sentence.

But the two sentences do not mean the same thing, necessarily. The first means that many people read very little, and the second means that only a few books are really popular. The point is that the movement of the actor or agent "people" from the front of the sentence to the end, an optional passive transformation, can change meaning. Sometimes the change is more subtle than the movement of the agent to the end of the sentence. For example, "The key opened the door" seems to have an active agent and an active verb ("The key opened"), but, in fact, the agent or person who actually opened the door is not to be found in the sentence.

Transformational grammar did not explain these variations in meaning very well because it insisted on separating and isolating syntax and meaning. Charles Fillmore's case grammar (1968) was one effort to establish the relationship between syntax and categories of meaning. In case grammar, noun phrases, in addition to their functions based on position in the sentence (subject, object, and so forth), have various semantic functions or cases:

1. Agent: *Bill* in "Bill opened the door" and "The door was opened by Bill"

2. Instrument: *Key* in "The key opened the door" and "The door was opened by the key"

3. Experiencer: *Bill* in "Bill is sick" and "Bill has a key"

4. Goal: *Bill* in "He gave the reward to Bill" and *key* in "Bill made the key"

5. Location: *Here* in "Bill was here"

6. Objective: *Door* in "The key opened the door" and *reward* in "He gave the reward to Bill"

This kind of analysis enables one to talk about how three quite different sentences are the same. In "I like books," "The books please me," and "The books are pleasing to me," *I* has the same case of *experiencer*, but different sentence positions. This analysis also provides for a way of talking about directness and clarity of style. Says Joseph Williams, "Since subjects and agents tend to coincide in the vast number of languages in the world, we might assume that their nexus is one of the 'natural ways' that reinforce what a sentence is about to express" (1979, 602). Williams then argues that the clearest style is one in which the agent and what it does are signaled by at least three grammatical structures—the grammatically defined roles of subject and predicate, the sequence of subject-agent first and what it does second, and the form classes of noun for subject-agent and verb for what the agent does.

Williams argues that "we need a theory of sentences in which clarity would be a concept we could not escape addressing" (32). He suggests that in the study of sentences we should begin with the case grammar and then examine how the case grammar or semantic structure matches the syntactic grammar. To Williams, clear sentences are those in which the case grammar agent is the syntactic grammar subject, the case grammar objective is the grammatical object, and so forth: "In short, the clearest style is one in which the grammatical structures of a sentence most redundantly support the perceived semantic structure." Williams (1979, 601) gives the example below (fig. 7) of match and mismatch between case grammar and syntactic grammar.

Williams's views about style are compatible with those of E. D. Hirsch, Jr., who argues that there are universal stylistic features in all good prose and that these features of good style are reducible to a single principle: "One prose style is better than another when it communicates the same meaning as the other but requires less effort from the reader" (Hirsch 1977, 9). He calls this principle "communicative efficiency" and "relative readability."

What is readable? Because experiments have shown that clauses in English are more directly perceived than their constituent words (Bever 1970), thus establishing the clause as the "primary perceptual unit" (Bever 1972), and because of the limits of short-term memory in storing units of information (Miller 1956), Hirsch argues that the crucial concept in readability is the concept of clause closure. Closure enables the reader to chunk the words into the single unit of the clause and to hold the structure in memory while reviewing meaning. Thus "That he had fallen into the pool was known by the whole class" is harder to read than "The whole class knew that he had fallen into the pool" because, according to Hirsch's theory of clarity, the second sentence gives us the clause structure at the very beginning ("The whole class knew that"), whereas

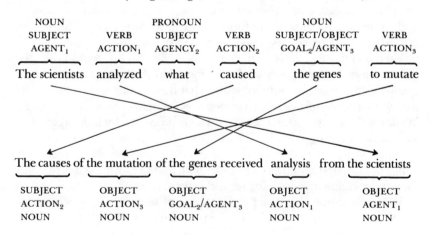

Figure 7. Match and mismatch between case grammar and syntactic grammar.

the first sentence postpones closure on the clause structure until the very end, requiring the reader to hold more individual pieces in short-term memory. Williams would say that the second sentence is clearer because the syntactic subject ("class") is the same as the case grammar agent.

Although the clause is recognized as the primary unit in most theories of clarity, the phrase is also recognized as a critical unit for chunking. Consider, for instance, which of the following is easier to recall immediately:

a. A leftward jaggedly descending curve
b. A jagged broken curve descending leftward

Various experiments suggest that the second one is easier to recall because the reader uses the subject "curve" to chunk words into units, "jagged broken curve" and "descending leftward." In *a*, the postponement of "curve" until the end prevents chunking into two units, and therefore short-term memory begins to get overloaded with four units, the four words before "curve." (If terms like short-term memory are unfamiliar, return to this section after reading chapter 3.)

But that is not the whole story. Rommetveit found that when subjects were given phrase *a* or *b* and asked to identify a picture of the curved line described in the phrase, subjects responding to *a* were more accurate than those responding to *b* (Rommetveit 1968, 287–300). Hirsch argues that these experiments suggest that language which is easy to process, such as the language in phrase *b*, does not necessarily do an accurate enough job of integrating material into a cohesive unit (Hirsch 1977, 115–16). Says Hirsch, "Again, we are led to the view that good stylistic choices are based upon intelligent compromises between conflicting psychological factors" (116)—readability or clarity, on the one hand, and an accurate integration of meaning, on the other. Although these various theories of clarity have given us some useful ways of thinking about language, they have not solved the problem that the application of many maxims of clarity do, in fact, change meaning.

Richard A. Lanham is one of those who has struggled with this problem. In his book on revision, he says (1979, viii):

> But when *do* you want to cure it? Students today often feel—sometimes with justification—that they will be penalized for writing plain English. In the academic bureaucracy, writing plain English seems like walking down the hall with nothing on. Such public places demand protective coloration. Furthermore, if you are going to write in The Official Style, how do you make sure you are writing a good and not a bad one? And if The Official Style is, all said and done, a bad prose style—and it is—what, then, can "good" and "bad" mean when applied to prose?

> *Revising Prose* starts out by teaching revision. When you've
> learned how to do that, we'll reflect on what such revision is likely to
> do for you—and to you—in the bureaucratic world of the future. We
> ought then to be able to see what "good" and "bad" mean for prose,
> and what you are really doing when you revise.

In his book on style, Lanham makes the following observation about
an example of obscurity (1974, 29–30):

> Taken in the abstract, in a stylistic universe of grace and ele-
> gance, such utterance makes a lover of prose long to slide into a
> warm bath and open a vein. For it is vintage bureaucratese. Yet, in
> context, it becomes both comprehensible and, in today's world of
> hokum, inevitable. The university this president directs had just
> learned of massive budget cuts—cuts, furthermore, coming for a
> second successive year after several lean years. . . .
>
> If you are telling a man he is going to take a cut in salary, that
> hard times are here again, you had better be long-winded, dismal,
> above all formal. That shows (1) that you *see* the gravity of the situ-
> ation, (2) that you *feel* the gravity of the situation as he does, (3) that
> you are the kind of sober and reliable fellow who can *deal with* the
> situation.

Lesson: Sentence Clarity

Among the important lessons in the language arts classroom are those
requiring students to rewrite hard-to-read sentences as more readable
ones. The following sentences from Ross Winterowd's *Contemporary
Writer* (1981, 461–62) are examples of the exercise and the rewrite:

> Whatever the family couldn't buy at the country store located at the
> crossroads five miles from town they *did without.*
>
> (The family *did without* whatever they couldn't buy at the country
> store located at the crossroads five miles from town.)
>
> The program was a concert of relatively pleasant newly discovered
> Appalachian dulcimer music.
>
> (The program was a concert of relatively pleasant dulcimer music
> that had been newly discovered in Appalachia.)
>
> To bake potatoes on an open bonfire, as we did when we were kids,
> was always a great *adventure.*
>
> (It was always a great *adventure* to bake potatoes on an open bonfire,
> as we did when we were kids.)

Joseph Williams is also concerned with how sentences end, arguing
that in exposition, at least, clear sentences tend to end with coordinate
structures, a nominalization, or a prepositional phrase introduced by *of.*
Lessons on structure often use contrasting pairs and ask students to select the better sentence in each pair and to explain their selections. Wil-

liams, for example, presents the following three pairs (1979, 607) to demonstrate the effect of the ending of the sentence. The lesson requires that the student identify in each pair which sentence is the original from W. Somerset Maugham, and which is the undesirable rewrite:

> I have never had much patience with the writers who claim from the reader an effort to understand their meaning.
>
> I have never had much patience with the writers who claim from the reader an effort to understand what they mean.
>
> Few people have written English with more grace than Berkeley.
>
> Few people have written English more gracefully than Berkeley.
>
> You would have thought that men who passed their lives in the study of the great masters of literature would be sufficiently sensitive to the beauty of language to write if not beautifully at least with perspecuity.
>
> You would have thought that men who passed their lives in the study of the great masters of literature would be sufficiently sensitive to the beauty of language to write if not beautifully at least perspicuously.

Topic and Test Conditions

A focus on clarity appears to require expository topics because passives tend to occur more frequently in expository prose. Williams says that narrative sentences do not show the same patterns in sentence endings. School assessors, therefore, should recognize that students who score well on narratives may still score poorly on exposition, because as the topic's demands become more complex students tend to backslide into problems they had previously solved. Many researchers believe that narratives based on personal experience do not require young writers to de-center, move away from an exclusive concern with themselves, that is, as much as does exposition based on society's problems and history, and thus demand less complexity.

Coding of Features

There are two indexes for agent-subject sentences. One is the percentage of clauses having an agent-subject match. In the three pairs below, the first sentence has the match, and the second does not:

> *I saw the movie./The movie was seen by me.*
>
> *The stars signaled the end./The stars were sign of the end.*
>
> *He discovered the secret in the book./The book revealed the secret to him.*

Active sentence index (% of clauses with agent-subject match)	=	$\dfrac{\text{Clauses with agent-subject match}}{\text{All clauses}}$

The other index of clarity and directness, according to Williams (1979, 607), is the frequency with which sentences end with (1) a coordinate structure, either within the last phrase or as the last phrase, (2) a nominalization (a noun derived from a verb or adjective, including gerunds), or (3) a prepositional phrase introduced by *of*. Says Williams, "Sentences that are both clear and strong are predominantly agent-action sentences, sentences that move briskly through relatively short subjects and verbs into a comment that climaxes with one of those three structures. (Narrative sentences do not reflect these distributions.)" (1979, 607)

Ending index (% of sentences with active ending)	=	$\dfrac{\text{Number of type of ending (coord/nom/prep)}}{\text{Total number of sentences}}$

Patterns of Use

The active sentence index for one ninth-grade reading was .92. Williams reports that clauses written in an emphatic and confident style end about two times out of every three with one of the three structures above (1979, 607). The counts below come from Williams's analysis of an article by Lee Edson ("The Advent of the Laser Age," *New York Times Magazine*, 26 March 1978, 34):

Some sub-totals: the number of sentences in Edson's article that end in comments with:

of:	22	15.6%	⎫
nominalizations:	22	15.6%	
coordination:	17	12.1%	
of + nomin.:	14	9.9%	⎬ 70.2%
of + coord.:	5	3.5%	
nomin. + coord.:	7	5%	
all three:	12	8.5%	⎭
none:	43	29.8%	

total *of:*	53
total nomin.:	55
total coord.:	41

Suggested Studies in Syntax

1. If longer NPs in the subject position suggest an increase in conceptual complexity, then do students with longer NPs read more? Beth Wiley, a teacher-researcher in the Bay Area Writing Project's credential program, examined a version of this question in a research project. She selected some writing samples for ranking the writing of the students in her class and then compared the general ranking of students as writers with the ranking of students on a norm-referenced language test (Wiley 1983). She found some interesting variations among the students, some students scoring low on the language test but high on the writing samples.

2. If students rank essays, do they give high scores to essays with high clarity indexes? The issue is whether students have adopted in their reading the standards of clarity suggested by Hirsch. Hirsch seems to believe that the easier something is to read, the better. Do young readers think so?

3 The Text

Bonnie Meyer (1982) has identified three levels of discourse organization: (1) the highlighting function (which helps a writer show a reader how some ideas are of greater importance than others); (2) the topical function (which helps both writer and reader conceive and organize main ideas on a topic); and (3) the informing function (which helps writer and reader make the transition from old to new information). In this chapter, the highlighting function is examined within the theory of the Christensens, the topical function is examined within various approaches to cohesive ties, and the informing function is examined within different global scales of text structure.

1 Feature: Highlighting Structures in the Text

Theory: Christensen Sequences

The work of Francis Christensen and Bonniejean Christensen (1978) on paragraph organization is an example of research focusing on highlighting functions. The Christensens argue that paragraphs are similar to what they call cumulative sentences in that paragraphs have, among other things, something like a base clause and levels of generality. The topic sentence is comparable to the base clause of a cumulative sentence because it is the structure to which all other sentences in the paragraph are added. The topic sentence is nearly always the first sentence of the paragraph. However, sometimes paragraphs do not have topic sentences, such as the following (Christensen and Christensen 1978, 93–94):

Paragraph without Topic Sentence

2 In Spain, where I saw him last, he looked profoundly Spanish.
   3 He might have passed for one of those confidential street dealers who earn their living selling spurious Parker pens in the cafés of Málaga or Valencia.
      4 Like them, he wore a faded chalk-striped shirt, a coat slung over his shoulders, a trim, dark moustache, and a sleazy, fat-cat smile.

4 His walk, like theirs, was a raffish saunter, and everything about him seemed slept in, especially his hair, a nest of small, wet serpents.
3 Had he been in Seville and his clothes been more formal, he could have been mistaken for a pampered elder son idling away a legacy in dribs and on drabs, the sort you see in windows along the Sierpes, apparently stuffed.
2 In Italy he looks Italian; in Greece, Greek: wherever he travels on the Mediterranean coast, Tennessee Williams takes on a protective colouring which melts him into his background, like a lizard on a rock.
2 In New York or London he seems out of place, and is best explained away as a retired bandit.
3 Or a beach comber: shave the beard off any of the self-portraits Gauguin painted in Tahiti, soften the features a little, and you have a sleepy outcast face that might well be Tennessee's.

                                        Kenneth Tynan, *Curtains*, p. 266

There are readers who think that the clause beginning with "wherever he travels" could be the topic sentence. The Christensens, however, want topic sentences at the beginning because for them topic sentences are little more than the beginning of a sequence of levels of generality. In the paragraph above, the levels of generality are shown by the numbers—the 2s referring to or modifying the 1, a 3 modifying a 2, and so forth. For example, the sentences that begin "In Spain," "In Italy," and "In New York" are on the same level of generality, and all have the same number—2. The fact that they all have 2s means that these sentences in the paragraph are coordinate with each other. There are two basic sequences of sentences—coordinate and subordinate (Christensen and Christensen 1978, 85, 82):

A. Coordinate Sequence

1 He [the native speaker] may, of course, speak a form of English that marks him as coming from a rural or an unread group.
2 But if he doesn't mind being so marked, there's no reason why he should change.
3 Samuel Johnson kept a Staffordshire burr in his speech all his life.
3 In Burns's mouth the despised Lowland Scots dialect served just as well as the "correct" English spoken by ten million of his southern contemporaries.
3 Lincoln's vocabulary and his way of pronouncing certain words were sneered at by many better educated people at the time, but he seemed to be able to use the English language as effectively as his critics.

                                        Bergen Evans, *Comfortable Words*, p. 6

B. Subordinate Sequence Paragraph

1 The process of learning is essential to our lives.
  2 All higher animals seek it deliberately.
    3 They are inquisitive and they experiment.
      4 An experiment is a sort of harmless trial run of some action which we shall have to make in the real world; and this, whether it is made in the laboratory by scientists or by fox-cubs outside their earth.
        5 The scientist experiments and the cub plays; both are learning to correct their errors of judgment in a setting in which errors are not fatal.
        6 Perhaps this is what gives them both their air of happiness and freedom in these activities.

The first paragraph is called *coordinate* because most of the sentences are at the same level of generality (all 3s) without any intervening subordinate sentences. The second paragraph is called *subordinate* because all of its sentences are at different levels of generality. From sentence 2 on, each sentence is subordinate to the previous one. Notice that sentences with the same number or level of generality have similar structures. According to the Christensens,

> Repetition of structure is necessary; like things in like ways is one of the imperatives of discursive writing. Any attempt to introduce variety in the sentence beginnings, by varying the pattern or by putting something before the subject, would be like trying to vary the columns of the Parthenon. In a subordinate sequence, just as clearly, repetition of structure must be avoided. Each added sentence, being different in method of development, must be different in form. (1978, 84)

The coordinate and subordinate sequences combine to produce the most common paragraph, the mixed sequence:

C. Mixed Sequence—Based on Coordinate Sequence

1 An obvious classification of meaning is that based on scope.
1 This is to say, meaning may be generalized (extended, widened) or it may be specialized (restricted, narrowed).
  2 When we increase the scope of a word, we reduce the elements of its contents.
    3 For instance *tail* (from OE *taegl*) in earlier times seems to have meant 'hairy caudal appendage, as of a horse.'
      4 When we eliminated the hairiness (or the horsiness) from the meaning, we increased its scope, so that in Modern English the word means simply 'caudal appendage.'
      4 The same thing has happened to Danish *hale*, earlier 'tail of a cow.'

     5 In course of time the cow was eliminated, and in
       present-day Danish the word means simply 'tail,'
       having undergone a semantic generalization pre-
       cisely like that of the English word cited;
    4 the closely related Icelandic *hali* still keeps the cow in
      the picture.
  3 Similarly, a *mill* was earlier a place for making things by the
    process of grinding, that is, for making meal. . . .

D. Mixed Sequence—Based on Subordinate Sequence

1 Science as we know it indeed is a creation of the last three
  hundred years.
2 It has been made in and by the world that took its settled
  shape about 1660, when Europe at last shook off the long
  nightmare of religious wars and settled into a life of in-
  quisitive trade and industry.
  Science is embodied in those new societies;
  it has been made by them and has helped to make them.
    4 The medieval world was passive and symbolic; it saw in
      the forms of nature the signatures of the Creator.
    4 From the first stirrings of science among the Italian
      merchant adventurers of the Renaissance, the mod-
      ern world has been an active machine.
      5 That world became the everyday world of trade in
        the seventeenth century and
        the interests were appropriately astronomy and the
        instruments of voyage, among them the magnet.
      5 A hundred years later, at the Industrial Revolution,
        the interest shifted to the creation and use of
        power.
        6 This drive to extend the strength of man and
          what he can do in a day's work has remained
          our interest since.
          7 In the last century it moved from steam to
            electricity.
          7 Then in 1905, in that wonderful year
            when . . . he published papers which made
            outstanding advances in three different
            branches of physics, Einstein first wrote
            down the equations which suggested that
            matter and energy are interchangeable
            states.
          7 Fifty years later, we command a reservoir of
            power in matter almost as large as the sun,
            which we now realize manufactures its heat
            for us in just this way, by the annihilation of
            its matter.

(J. Bronowski, *The Common Sense of Science* [Cambridge: Harvard
Univ. Press, 1978], 97–98)

Lesson: Levels of Generality

Traditional teaching approaches to discourse organization usually emphasized the topical function (the thesis sentence), but the Christensens' new rhetoric shifted the emphasis from the topical function to highlighting. The Christensens, in fact, argued that the thesis sentence was simply the first sentence and that the relationship among the sentences—subordinate, coordinate, and mixed—was the key organizational pattern in discourse, not what was first. Their approach generated a number of textbooks and teaching approaches still used in K–12 classrooms.

The lessons on levels of generality ask students to identify those levels in a given paragraph, to invent the sentences that might be written at different levels of an assigned paragraph structure, and to extend the analysis of levels of generality to whole essays, treating each paragraph as one level in a sequence. The work of James Gray and Robert Benson (1982) gives other examples. The following selection from a Benson lesson (35) illustrates what happens:

> In asking the students to build a subordinate sequence paragraph, I have them go back to the previous topic: "Why are you in college?" Earlier it had discouraged them, but this time they are aided by the visual image of a series of sentences connected by a sequence of descending levels, each sentence leading on logically to the next. "It's like going downstairs," I tell them, and the object in this exercise is to go down as far as possible, to establish an unbroken sequence of thought, to follow the route suggested by each sentence as it is written.

> Why am I here? I am here because I am really getting bored with the post office. I work in the mail sort room, and this means you spend all your time sorting and carrying mail. I have to carry 50 pound sacks of mail and dump them onto a conveyor belt for two hours a day. I don't mind hard work, but can't you imagine yourself after twenty years of abuse to your back? You would be next in line for the Quasimodo look-alike contest. I want out, and school is a good way to escape. If I get a degree, I might have a better chance of finding a job that doesn't require so much physical exertion. I guess you could say I'm in school to save my aching back.

> —Rafael Gonzales

Topic and Test Conditions

Some topics are thought to be more likely to generate particular sequences. For example, in narrative topics, students often use many coordinate sequences arranged in chronological order—*and, and then,* and so forth. The best way to test what is likely to happen with a given topic is to have teachers and a selected group of students write on the topic and then apply a selected method of feature analysis.

Coding of Levels of Generality

The coding of levels of generality has two approaches. For many teachers, the encouragement of paragraph development, no matter what kind, is a central purpose of instruction, and for these teachers the average number of sentences per paragraph and the number of paragraphs are useful indicators of paragraph development. In this index, however, the sentences could be short and the overall organization confused.

$$\text{Paragraph development indicator} = \frac{\text{Total number of sentences}}{\text{Total number of paragraphs}} \Big/ \text{Number of paragraphs}$$

Another indicator of paragraph development is the index of levels of generality. This index adds together the numbers marking the level of generality of each sentence and divides the total by the number of sentences in the paragraph, giving the average level of generality in the paragraph. If more than one paragraph is to be indexed, then the indexes for each paragraph are added together and divided by the number of paragraphs.

LG = Levels of generality for the paragraph

$$\text{LG index (average) for paragraph} = \frac{\text{Total of LG numbers in paragraph}}{\text{Total sentences in paragraph}}$$

LG = Levels of generality for the essay

$$\text{LG index (average) for essay} = \frac{\text{Total of LG indexes for each paragraph}}{\text{Total number of paragraphs in essay}}$$

For example, the LG Index for the coordinate paragraph *a* on page 44 is calculated as follows:

Total of LG numbers in paragraph *a*: 1,2,3,3,3 = 12
Divided by total number of sentences: LG Total: 12

Divided by 5 sentences

LG index for paragraph *a*: 12 divided by 5 sentences = 2.4

The LG index for an essay composed of paragraphs *b, c,* and *d* is calculated as follows:

LG index for *b:* 21 divided by 6 sentences = 3.5

LG index for *c:* 20 divided by 7 sentences = 2.8

LG index for *d:* 44 divided by 10 sentences = 4.4

Total of LGs for each paragraph: 3.5 + 2.8 + 4.4 = 10.7 divided by 3 (number of paragraphs) = 3.5

The approaches discussed thus far have had two means of judging paragraph development, length of the paragraph calculated in average number of sentences per paragraph, and average level of generality in the paragraph or essay. But counts are not the only way to study paragraph development. Counts provide one kind of description of paragraphs, but the counts themselves do not necessarily mean anything. An average level of generality of 2, for example, representing very little subordination, is neither good nor bad in itself. More global considerations are at work when value judgments are made. Instead of counts, Rebekah Caplan, a teacher in the Bay Area Writing Project, and Catherine Keech, a research assistant in the project, used a general impression scale to index coordinate and subordinate sequences or levels of generality. Their study, examining the effects of a writing program emphasizing the importance of concrete detail, coded sequences of abstract and concrete detail. In addition to holistically scoring the writing samples, readers ranked each sentence in the student essays as (1) highly abstract, (2) more focused generalization, (3) somewhat generally stated detail or example offered, and (4) specific, concrete detail, image, or event. The range of movement among levels of abstraction was calculated by subtracting the top (most abstract) level from the bottom (most concrete) level used by the student (e.g., 4 − 1 = 3). The two examples below show samples of student writing from Caplan and Keech's study (1980, 129–31), their holistic scores for the writing, the scales for the levels of abstraction, the sentence analysis chart, and the commentary on each paper:

Topic A—Holistic Score: 4 + 4 = 8

(1) "Get off that box!" (2) A day doesn't go by that I don't hear those words. (3) "The Box" or "The idiot box" are the ways my parents define the word television set. (4) The fighting and arguing always starts because of my little brother who watches an overwhelming amount of T.V., at least four hours everyday. (5) It is amazing how much time he has to waste watching everything that flashes on the screen from "Hawaii five-0" to "Big Time Wrestling" while I hardly find the time to watch one program per week.

(6) All those comercials and programs that clog his mind; also have a great deal of influence over him. (7) Programs such as "The Streets of San Francisco" and "Starsky and Hutch" teach a child about violence, robbery, rape and many other crimes.

(8) Many advertisements also are a bad influence. (9) The ciggarette comericals teach that smoking is glamorus and the junk food comericals, especially the cerials teach the younger minds that eating sugar coated pink and green shapes can be good for you.

(10) Commercials like these can throw a child off as far as reality is concerend not to metion the eaquily bad influence of television programs.

Level of Abstraction Analysis

Number of Different Abstraction Levels Used: Top Level __2__
Bottom Level __4__
Total Range __2__

Sentence Number:

	1	2	3	4	5	6	7	8	9	10	11	12	13	14	15	16	17	18	19	20	21	22
1																						
2				X		X		X														
3							X		X													
4	X	X	X	X	X				↓													

CONCRETE ABSTRACT

This paper is interesting in two respects. First, it begins with a concrete episode and direct quotations—quite effective in this case. Second, it never quite reaches level one, a full statement of the thesis the essay is arguing. Sentence ten comes closest to filling that function. In spite of—or because of—this rather atypical approach to argument, the paper was scored as an upper-half paper. Sentence nine stands out for its use of details which make children's cereals *sound* poisonous without ever making that claim.

Topic A—Holistic Score: 5 + 5 = 10

(1) The greatest thing about the United States is the freedom offered here. (2) Everyone has freedom of choice. (3) Television is one example of freedom of choice. (4) No one is forced to watch a program or not to watch another. (5) Even though some television programs display violence or sex, it is the right of every citizen to decide what they want to see. (6) A program can not influence anyone unless they desire it to.

(7) Many shows, for example. Kojak and Barretta, show its viewers violent street crime. (8) These could be considered an influence of how one is not supposed to act and not necessarily lead them on to copy these examples. (9) However, like most decisions in life, some will choose to follow the "wrong path".

(10) These people are only wrongly influenced because it was their choice, (11) no one forced them to sit in front of the tube at 8:30 and watch chanel whatever.

(12) Critics complain frequently about the content of television programs. (13) They, however, seem not to take into consideration the education offered in some such as Sesame Street and Teens today. (14) From these, large numbers of children in the United States have undoubtedly benefited.

(15) Television can be considered good or bad depending on which programs and what outlooks one takes. (16) Everyone is free to switch it off if they feel a flick not worthy. (17) Television's influence only depends on the individual.

Level of Abstraction Analysis

Number of Different Abstraction Levels Used: Top Level __1 –__
Bottom Level __3 +__
Total Range __3__

Sentence Number:

CONCRETE ABSTRACT		1	2	3	4	5	6	7	8	9	10	11	12	13	14	15	16	17	18	19	20	21	22
	1	X	X	X	X		X									X	X	X					
	2					X↑X			X	X	X	X	X		X		↓X						
	3							X						↓		X							
	4																						

This paper appeared difficult to analyze at first, because the introductory sentences about "freedom of choice," if classified as level one, pushed all the following sentences down one level in comparison with similar sentences in other student essays. Sentences three and four "Television is one example of freedom of choice. No one is forced to watch a program . . ." begin the discussion of television itself, which is where most other papers commence. Raters solved the problem by classifying sentences one and two as more abstract than the frame. As a result, although the student does not use level four sentences, he can be said to have a total range that crosses three level-boundaries.

In this context, sentences four, six and sixteen say much the same thing. Sixteen is classified as slightly more concrete because of the qualifying clause, "if they feel a flick is not worthy."

Patterns of Use

Teacher-researchers who wish to compare their findings with the findings of others will find the norms in the area of paragraph development somewhat obscure. First, many studies do not present student examples to illustrate what is being discussed. Second, paragraph development has not attracted as much research interest as has syntax. However, some patterns are available. One study of paragraph length in academic articles found a mean (average) of 5.0 sentences per paragraph, a standard deviation of 1.6, and a range from 1.7 to 11.0 (Broadhead, Berlin, and Broadhead 1982, 231). One ninth-grade reading showed an average paragraph length of 3.5 sentences per paragraph for high papers and 1.3 for low papers. The index of levels of generality for these ninth-grade papers was 1.9 for high papers and 1.2 for low papers.

2 Feature: Cohesive Ties

Theory: Cohesion

The traditional view has been that the next unit above the sentence was the text and that the text could come in the form of one or more paragraphs, which usually had two or more sentences each. The Christensens' theory of sequences represents one effort to describe intersentential relationships in terms of some definitive unit of analysis. Cohesion theory represents a second effort. Cohesion refers to "text-forming relations" (Halliday and Hasan 1976, 7), and its primary unit of analysis is the cohesive tie.

W. Ross Winterowd has identified seven types of ties, each expressing a different relationship (Winterowd 1975, 229–30):

> *Coordination* can always be expressed by *and*. (Synonyms: *furthermore, in addition, too, also, again,* etc.)
>
> Boswell was a Rousseau-ite, one of the first of the Romantics, an inveterate sentimentalist, *AND* nothing could be more complete than the contrast between his career and Gibbon's.
>
> —*Lytton Strachey*
>
> They almost hid from us the front, but through the dust and the spaces between running legs we could see the soldiers in the trench leap their barricade like a breaking wave. *AND* then the impenetrable dust shut down *AND* the fierce stabbing needle of the machine guns sewed the mighty jumble of sounds together.
>
> —*John Reed*
>
> . . . Marat is, in most of his speeches, tinsel, stage scenery, or an element in a great painting. *AGAIN,* the Brechtian songs are touching, but ironically and allusively touching; Charlotte Corday, the mad, beautiful country girl mouthing her lines, is *AGAIN* an element in a picture, an aesthetic contrivance.
>
> —*Stuart Hampshire*
>
> *Obversativity* can always be expressed by *but*. (Synonyms: *yet, however, on the other hand,* etc.)
>
> It has been ambitious and plucky of me to attempt to describe what is indescribable, and I have failed, as I knew I would. *BUT* I have discharged my duty to society. . . .   —*E. B. White*

And Johnson, as Kennedy has often acknowledged, was a man of force and decision to whom, in case anything happened, the government could responsibly be assigned.

ON THE OTHER HAND, the designation of Johnson would outrage the liberal wing of the party.   —*Arthur Schlesinger, Jr.*

Causativity can always be expressed by *for.* It is interesting to note that among the transitional adverbs commonly used (nevertheless, however, moreover, hence, consequently, nonetheless, accordingly, then, besides, likewise, indeed, therefore), none expresses the causative relationship.

Now, on that morning, I stopped still in the middle of the block, *FOR* I'd caught out of the corner of my eye a tunnel-passage, an overgrown courtyard.   —*Truman Capote*

Conclusivity can always be expressed by *so.* (Synonyms: *therefore, thus, for this reason,* etc.)

She has a rattling Corsican accent, likes Edith Piaf records, and gives me extra shrimp bits in my shrimp salad. *SO* some things change. Last time I heard no Edith Piaf and earned no extra forkfuls of shrimp.   —*Herbert Gold*

Alternativity can always be expressed by *or.*

Now such an entity, even if it could be proved beyond dispute, would not be God: it would merely be a further piece of existence, that might conceivably not have been there—*OR* a demonstration would not have been required.   —*John A. T. Robinson*

Inclusivity is often expressed with a *colon.*

In the first century B.C., Lucretius wrote this description of the pageant of Cybele:

Adorned with emblem and crown . . . she is carried in awe-inspiring state. . . .   —*Harvey Cox*

The inclusive relationship is that of the example to the generality or the narration of the case to the statement of the case. Often, inclusivity is expressed by the transformational possibility of complementization:

He realized that their discovery [Aristotle's discovery of the statues of Daedalus] would shatter his own "natural" law: Managers would no longer need subordinates, masters could dispense with slaves.   —*Michael Harrington*

With the last two clauses complementized, the sentence reads like this:

He realized that their discovery would shatter his own "natural" law, that managers would no longer need subordinates, and that masters could dispense with slaves.

The *sequential relationship* is expressed by such transitions as "first . . . second . . . third," "earlier . . . later," "on the bottom . . . in the middle . . . on top," and so on.

Winterowd's list is not conclusive. In the system of M. A. K. Halliday and Ruqaiya Hasan (1976), there are five major types of cohesive ties—

substitution, ellipsis, reference, lexical, and conjunction—and many of Winterowd's transitions are examples of *conjunction*. Halliday and Hasan's *conjunction* comes in four forms (1976, 238–39):

> *additive*: and, or, besides
>> For the whole day he climbed. *And* he met no one.
> *adversative*: but, yet, however, on the other hand, nevertheless
>> *Yet* he was hardly aware of being tired.
> *causal*: so, because, if/then
>> *So* by evening he had left his camp far below him.
> *temporal*: next, then, after, first, finally, soon
>> *Then* he sat down to rest.

The other four major types of cohesion also come in various forms. The most frequent type of *reference* is the use of pronouns, and a common *substitution* is *one* ("Two men have just arrived. The first *one* you know"). *Ellipsis* is the dropping of words that are understood ("Metal stocks will not fall. Neither will electronics [fall]"). Finally, *lexical* cohesion is the use of synonyms and the repetition of words.

Most ties have a dimension of directionality, referring back *(anaphora)* or forward *(cataphora)* in the text. This trait of forward and backward directionality is one indicator of stylistic variety in paragraph development. There is also the reference outside of the text *(exophora)*, such as Fillmore's famous example of the note in the bottle which washes up on shore: "Meet me here tomorrow with a stick about this big." These outside references often have a deictic function, putting writer and reader in the same situational space. These dimensions will be discussed in more detail in the chapter on social context.

In addition to directionality, Halliday and Hasan's cohesive ties have a text-span dimension with four different classes. Witte and Faigley (1981, 194–95) give the following description of how to classify a student's text span:

> *Text-Span Classes (Immediate, Mediated, Remote, Mediated-Remote)*
>
> (31) *Respect* is one reason people change their behavior.
> (32) For example, one does not speak with his *boss* as he would talk to a friend or co-worker.
> (33) One might use four-letter words in talking to a co-worker, but probably not in talking to his *boss*.
> (34) In talking to teachers or *doctors*, people also use bigger words than normal.
> (35) Although the situation is different than when one speaks with a *boss* or a *doctor*, one often talks with a minister or priest different [sic] than he talks with friends or *family*.
> (36) With the *family*, most people use a different language when they talk to parents or grandparents than when they talk to younger brothers and sisters.

(37) People's ability to use language in different ways allows them to show the *respect* they should toward different people, whether they are professionals, *family* members, clergy, friends and co-workers, or *bosses.*

Immediate cohesive ties semantically linked adjacent T-units. The repetition of *doctor* in sentences (34) and (35) creates an *immediate* tie, forcing the reader to assimilate the content of (34) into the content of (35). In contrast, the repetition of *family* in sentences (35), (36), and (37) forms a *mediated* tie. The semantic bridge established by the occurrence of *family* in (35) and (37) is channelled through or mediated by the repetition of *family* in (36). The cohesive tie involving the repetition of *family* is not simply a series of immediate ties, because once a lexical item appears in a text all subsequent uses of that item presuppose the first appearance. *Immediate* and *mediated* ties join items in adjacent T-units. Such ties enable writers to introduce a concept in one T-unit and to extend, modify, or clarify that concept in subsequent and successive T-units.

Remote ties, on the other hand, result when the two elements of a tie are separated by one or more intervening T-units. The tie between *respect* in (31) and (37) is *remote;* here the repetition of the word signals to the reader that the semantic unit represented by the paragraph is now complete. Finally, ties which are both mediated and remote are called *mediated-remote.* An example of this type of cohesive tie appears in the repetition of *bosses* in sentences (32), (33), (35), and (37). Here the presupposing *bosses* in (37) is separated from the presupposed *boss* in (32) by intervening T-units (34) and (36) which contain no element relevant to the particular cohesive tie. Thus the tie is *remote.* However, the presupposing *bosses* is also *mediated* through repetitions of *boss* in (33) and (35). Hence the term *mediated-remote.* Skilled writers use mediated-remote ties to interweave key "themes" within the text.

Theories of cohesive ties generally argue that ties can indicate a writer's linguistic resources for idea development. A number of reservations have been expressed, however, about the present state of cohesion theory. For example, some researchers have argued that Halliday and Hasan should have included parallelism as an indicator because parallelism often creates a cohesive tie, creating a relationship, as the Christensens have said, by repeating structure (Witte and Faigley 1981, 200). A second argument says the ties are markers of cohesion, not its creators. If there is not already some lexical compatibility, then the presence of a cohesion marker cannot establish a relationship. The question remains, therefore, what the source of cohesion actually is. One result of the debate over cohesion is the view that cohesion (and its ties) are not the same as coherence (Witte and Faigley 1981, 199). Cohesion refers to explicit mechanisms in the text—for example, cohesive ties, parallelism, verb tense—and coherence refers to conditions that allow a text to be understood in a real-world setting. Some of these conditions will be the subject of the next section.

Another criticism of present theory of cohesive ties is that most counts of ties and their classification ignore the location of each tie. Joseph Williams, for one, has argued (1985) that the location of old and new information is a critical feature of text cohesion. In his view of the cohesive text, the sentence should typically begin with "old" information, that is, information introduced at the end of the previous sentence, and then move to new information.

Lesson: Connecting Text

Most composition books have lessons on transitions. One common approach is to give students a rewritten paragraph in which some of the transition words have been changed to illogical and incorrect selections and ask the students to find the transitions that do not work. Ken Davis's use of the cloze test as a diagnostic tool for revision is another interesting way to teach awareness of cohesive ties and their function in the text (1982, 121). In this exercise each student prepares a cloze test by counting back fifty to one hundred words from the end of the essay. The point is that the test should begin after the first five to ten lines, depending on the total length of the essay. For younger children, a shorter beginning will be needed. Then in the section counted the student should underline every fifth, seventh, or tenth word and recopy the essay, substituting numbered blanks for the underlined words. Finally, the student should prepare a chart like that below, which will accompany the recopied essay with its blanks. Then the chart and essay circulate among readers who must fill in the chart with guesses about what word is missing from the blank. Result: readers must look for clues, often in the form of cohesive ties, about what the missing words might be. Writers have the readers' guesses returned to them, allowing them to calculate how predictable the text was. (See Davis's article for a good follow-up discussion with examples.)

Blank #	Your word	Reader 1	Reader 2	Reader 3	H or M	+ or −
1						
2						

Joseph Williams presents another kind of lesson examining the cohesiveness of texts. He begins with illustrations of his two principles of order and emphasis, defining the relationship of old and new information in a cohesive text:

> *Whenever possible, express at the beginning of a sentence ideas already stated, referred to, implied, safely assumed, familiar, predictable, less important, readily accessible information.*

The other principle is this:

> *Express at the end of a sentence the least predictable, the most important, the most significant information, information you almost certainly want to emphasize.*

Then he introduces several paragraphs which may violate these two principles and asks the student to revise where necessary.

Topic and Test Conditions

Teacher-researchers must remember, as always, that topic and test conditions can influence the use of cohesive ties. Bonnie Meyer's notion of five basic writing plans (Meyer 1982) suggests that some topics will, in fact, encourage the use of some kinds of transitions and discourage the use of others. Similarly, Stephanie Gray and Catherine Keech, teacher consultants in the Bay Area Writing Project, found that lessons emphasizing comparison topics produced an increased use of *-er* adverbs *(longer, faster, better)* and such terms and phrases as *whereas, on the other hand,* and *as . . . as* (1980).

Coding of Features of Coherence

One formula used as an index of ties is a count of the ties divided by the total number of words in a text.

$$\text{Cohesive ties index (ratio of cohesive ties to total words)} = \frac{\text{Markers of coherence by type (reference, substitution, etc.)}}{\text{Total words}}$$

This index assumes that the frequency of ties is an indicator of the writer's improvement in understanding paragraph development. For some students in some classrooms, this assumption may be correct. Another formula used is a count of cohesive ties divided by the total number of T-units, the result multiplied by 100. The teacher-researcher, of course, must explain the basis for selecting whatever index is used.

$$\text{Tie /T-unit index (cohesive ties per 100 T-units)} = \frac{\text{Total number of cohesive ties (by type)}}{\text{Total number of T-units}} \times 100$$

The index above assumes that the use of ties must not be restricted to connecting clauses (T-units), but must include connections within the clause. Another index is a count of the text-span classes described by Witte and Faigley. I have never tried this count in a school district assessment, but I have been told by teacher-researchers that it is useful.

$$\text{Index of text-span types} = \frac{\text{Total number of a given type of text span (immediate, mediated, remote, mediated-remote)}}{\text{Total of all types of text span}}$$

The various indexes of cohesive ties are not as clearcut as they at first seem. The coding of ellipsis and lexical ties, for example, can be very difficult for readers with little experience with the concept. Ellipsis needs to be given a very limited definition. Say Halliday and Hasan, "When we talk of ellipsis, we are not referring to any and every instance in which there is some information that the speaker has to supply from his own evidence. . . . We are referring to sentences, clauses, etc., whose structure is such as to presuppose some preceding item, which then serves as the source of the missing information. An elliptical item is one which leaves specific structural slots to be filled from elsewhere" (1976, 143).

The problem is that some coders will say that the sentence "We left" is an example of ellipsis because a previous sentence makes clear what structural slot follows "left." That is, it was "the home" which was left, for example. This interpretation opens ellipsis to very diverse coding. Teachers who code ellipsis should list many examples on the coding sheet, showing what counts and what does not.

A restricted definition and extensive training are also needed to code lexical cohesion. Halliday and Hasan have outlined the difficulties involved, concluding that "the concept of the lexical item is not totally clearcut; like most linguistic categories, although clearly defined in the ideal, it presents many indeterminacies in application to actual instances" (1976, 292). A restricted definition of lexical cohesion, making more reliable coding possible, is: "Lexical cohesion includes instances of repeating the same word, synonyms *(apple* for *fruit, peak* for *top of the mountain)*, closely related pairs representing a contrast *(wet/dry, boys/girls)* or sequence *(joke/laugh, morning/afternoon/night)* or parts of the same set *(north/south, blue/red, door/window)*."

Patterns of Use

Four examples of studies of coherence are presented here. In the 1980 Gray and Keech study, students who were given extensive practice writing comparison essays increased their use of *as* words *(whereas, on the other hand, however, as . . . as),* as shown in the ratio of *as* words to total words—from .0153 to .0233 in eleventh grade and from .0149 to .0294 in ninth grade (42).

Second, in a study of the writing of college freshmen, Cooper et al. (1979) found that comparatives were more frequent in the writing of the best writers. They report that such expressions as *same as, similar to, different from,* and *better* or *worse than* were not present in the writing of the weakest writers. The best writers, however, used approximately 10 such comparatives for every 100 T-units. Substitution and ellipsis did not appear at all in papers by weak writers, and the best writers used substitution 2.90 times per 100 T-units and ellipsis 1.45 times. The use of conjunction per 100 T-units was 17.39 for the most competent and 16.36 for the least competent. The most striking differences in lexical cohesion occurred in synonyms. The strongest writers used 11.59 synonyms per 100 T-units, and the writing of the least competent writers had no ties whatsoever resulting from the use of synonyms.

Third, in a study of tenth-grade writing, Ken Lane, Sandra Murphy, and Kathleen Berry (1981) found the following distribution of Halliday and Hasan's four types of conjunctions:

Additive	*Causal*	*Adversative*	*Temporal*
49.80	11.27	15.57	23.36

They also found that writers in the low-scoring group averaged 5.06 additive ties per 100 words, but writers in the middle range of scores averaged 3.80 and writers in the high group averaged 3.36 additive ties per 100 words.

On text span and other indexes, Witte and Faigley report the following results from an analysis of ten essays written by college freshmen (1981, 196):

> The ways in which writers of the high- and low-rated essays form cohesive ties also distinguish the two groups of five essays from each other. Writers of the high-rated essays use a substantially higher relative percentage of *immediate* (High: 41.6%/Low: 32.8%) and *mediated* (High: 7.6%/Low: 0.8%) cohesive ties than do the writers of the low-rated essays. On the other hand, writers of the low-rated essays use more *mediated-remote* (High: 25.9%/Low: 36.7%) and *remote* ties (High: 26.9%/Low: 29.7%). These percentages allow us to focus on some crucial differences between the two essay sets. The larger relative percentage of *immediate* cohesive ties in the high-rated essays suggests, among other things, that the better writers tend to establish stronger cohesive bonds between individual T-units than do the writers of the low-rated essays. Analyses of *reference* and *conjunctive cohesion* support this observation. Writers of high-rated essays employ reference cohesion about twice as often, 84.1 times to

47.8 times per 100 T-units, as the writers of low-rated papers. The largest difference in the occurrence of referential cohesion is reflected in the higher frequency of third-person pronouns in the high-rated essays (High: 25.1 per 100 T-units/Low: 5.1 per 100 T-units). This lower frequency of third-person pronouns in the low-rated essays may be a direct result of the less skilled writers' attempts to avoid errors such as ambiguous pronoun reference. Because third-person pronouns usually refer back to the T-unit immediately preceding, we can infer that the writers of high-rated essays more often elaborate, in subsequent and adjacent T-units, topics introduced in a given T-unit.

They also add to their report the following kind of descriptive approach to cohesion (a comment on a high-rated paper):

> It is a job that really changes our behavior. Among other changes, we change the way we dress. In many jobs college graduates want to look responsible and mature, projecting an image of competence. The college student who wore faded blue jeans is now in three-piece suits. He feels the need to be approved of and accepted by his boss and associates. While he talked of socialism in college, he now reaps the profits of capitalism. While in college he demanded honesty in the words and actions of others, on the job he is willing to "kiss ass" to make friends or get a promotion. Indeed, working can change behavior.

Notice that in the paragraph [above] from the high-rated paper, *behavior* is repeated only one time. Yet the reader never questions that the paragraph is about changes in behavior. The writer repeatedly supplies examples of types of behavior, which are linked to the topic by a series of lexical collocations (e.g., *behavior, dress, look responsible, blue jeans, three-piece suits*). Clearly, the paragraph from the high-rated paper extends the semantic domain of the concept *behavior* to include a number of differentiated lexical items. Low-rated papers rarely show such extended series of collocations.

3 Feature: Global Impressions of Text

Theory: Organizational Structure and Analytical Scoring

A number of scholars have serious reservations about the use of counts to describe the structures of texts. These scholars argue first that some sentences have relationships unmarked by a given cohesive tie. For instance, the two sentences "He wanted to win the prize. He did not get it." have between them an unstated "but." In this case, a count would not reveal structure.

A second argument is that the structure of a text is often defined by a relationship among several structures, not just the matching of one. The mind helps locate the meaning in the text, inserting such things as the "but," by making various guesses about the relationships among several overall structures that are used as guides but that rarely appear in pure form in actual texts. For example, Bonnie Meyer's five basic writing plans—antecedent/consequent, comparison, description, response, and time-order—sometimes appear in combination with one another. One plan may be primary but other plans also appear.

In addition, the question of what is basic is itself an estimate of priorities. Frank J. D'Angelo (1975), for example, seems to use a sense of movement as the categorical principle, dividing structure into (1) static, (2) progressive, (3) repetitive, and (4) nonlogical. The static structures are description and classification; the progressive structures are narration, process, and cause-effect; and the repetitive structures are the enumeration or listing of items and the movement between negative and positive assertions. Josephine Miles (1979) has a different list of patterns of organization, giving priority to the parallels between sentence grammar and text in her categories. She sees the subject-predicate relationship in the sentence as similar to the topic-organizational development relationship in text structure. She also says that "one of the simplest ways to observe and follow significant order . . . is to pay close attention to the connectives in the passage" (27). Her list includes additives (like *and* and *then*), comparatives *(as)*, disjunctives *(but)*, alternatives *(on the other hand)*, causal subordinates *(if)*, descriptive subordinates *(who)*, and temporal and spatial locatives *(where)*. Like others, Miles warns that the connectives do not tell the whole story. Word order and sentence position are also important: "In composition, the selection of material is supported and conditioned by the ordering of the material, its position, and the devices signalling order, the connectives" (27).

How does one analyze organizational structures that cannot be counted? Paul B. Diederich's analytic scale (1974) is one answer. This scale assumes that one can identify the distinct qualities of good writing and select out these qualities for individual ratings. Diederich recommends that beginning readers, in assessing writing, should give rankings for ideas, organization, wording, and flavor. Each item is accompanied by a description of high, medium, and low qualities and sometimes by sample papers illustrating that item, with a score. After some experience reading and scoring papers on particular criteria, readers, according to Diederich, should be able to "move easily and naturally into the use of standard scores . . . rating on general impression" (55). "General impression scoring" means the same as holistic scoring. Because these days many teachers have had experience reading papers in controlled situations, many school districts reverse the order Diederich recommends. After holistic scores are given, teachers assign scores

for organization, coherence, ideas, and any information that is important to the writing curriculum.

Another assumption of Diederich's analytic scale is that the organization and cohesion issues will be fundamentally the same in all papers.
This is not necessarily the case. For this reason, scales and their descriptions are sometimes prepared for each reading.

Part of the theoretical support for scales like Diederich's comes from
the work of C. E. Osgood, G. J. Suci, and P. H. Tannenbaum (1957) with
the semantic differential. In their scale, subjects were to characterize
such things as *Father* (26):

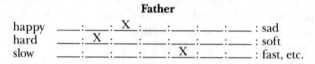

Father

happy	——:——: X :——:——:——:—— : sad
hard	——: X :——:——:——:——:—— : soft
slow	——:——:——:——: X :——:—— : fast, etc.

In the above test, *father* is described as "slightly happy, quite hard, and
slightly fast." The scale provides a way for turning words into relative
numbers and turning the numbers into a semantic average. Osgood and
his collaborators sampled responses to such scales from given speech
communities and treated the degree of agreement among answers as a
significant and measurable variable distinguishing one group from
another.

This procedure is quite similar to the way analytic scales are used.
First of all, the scales themselves have rankings from "good" to "poor"
on such matters as organization, very much like the scale from "happy"
to "sad" above. Furthermore, when readers use the scales to score anchor papers, they are developing a semantic average for organization in
those papers, and this average is intended to control the readings of individual readers so that they score features in the same way. Differences
from one set of anchor papers to another distinguish among points on
the ranking scale.

Lesson, Topic, and Test Conditions

A common lesson emphasizing global judgments is the use of scrambled
paragraphs. Well-written paragraphs are scrambled, and students are
asked to put the sentences in order. Then the class discusses the reasons
for the various versions. Another lesson is the modeling or imitation lesson (Myers and Gray 1983, 15–18). In general, the lessons and conditions
of tests and topics are the same as those mentioned in previous sections
of this chapter.

Coding of Organizational Structures

Different scales are used for the scoring of distinct structures. Below is a scale from Diederich (1974, 54–57).

Topic _____ Reader _____ Paper _____					
	Low		Middle		High
Ideas	2	4	6	8	10
Organization	2	4	6	8	10
Wording	1	2	3	4	5
Flavor	1	2	3	4	5 _____
Usage	1	2	3	4	5
Punctuation	1	2	3	4	5
Spelling	1	2	3	4	5
Handwriting	1	2	3	4	5 _____
				Sum	_____

Readers who use Diederich's scale total ideas, organization, wording, and flavor and then total usage, punctuation, spelling, and handwriting. These two totals are then added together. Before using the scale, readers must discuss what the various terms mean, and the resulting definitions must then be recorded and distributed. Below are examples of definitions for low and high scores in ideas and organization:

Ideas

High—The student has given some thought to the topic and writes what he really thinks.

Low—It is either hard to tell what points the student is trying to make or else they are so silly that . . . .

Organization

High—The paper starts at a good point, has a sense of movement, gets somewhere, and then stops.

Low—This paper starts anywhere and never gets anywhere.

Another kind of scale is one developed by the National Assessment of Educational Progress (1980, 1:32) for cohesion.

Cohesion Scoring Guide Categories

1 = *Little or no evidence of cohesion:* clauses and sentences are not connected beyond pairings.

2 = *Attempts at cohesion:* evidence of gathering details but little or no evidence that these details are meaningfully ordered. Very little would seem lost if the details were rearranged.

3 = *Cohesion:* details are both gathered and ordered. Cohesion does not necessarily lead to coherence, to the successful binding of parts so that the sense of the whole discourse is greater than the sense of its parts. In pieces of writing that are cohesive rather than coherent, there are large sections of details that cohere but these sections stand apart as sections.

4 = *Coherence:* while there may be a sense of sections within the piece of writing, the sheer number and variety of cohesion strategies bind the details and sections into a wholeness. This sense of wholeness can be achieved by a saturation of syntactic repetition throughout the piece and/or by closure that retrospectively orders the entire piece and/or by general statements that organize the whole piece.

The following is an example of a scale designed to identify organizational qualities associated with a particular topic—in this case, a compare and contrast essay. The developers felt that the scale represented a hierarchy of skill in organizing a particular topic, with the highest level "appearing to arise out of the use of experimental materials by more able students" (Gray and Keech 1980, 35).

Compare/Contrast Scale

0 = no apparent organization, random association of ideas or confusing changes of direction. (a)

1 = "integrated" or point-by-point comparison; usually three to seven sentences listing differences or similarities between the items being compared or contrasted; no development or larger framework of organization. (b, c, d)

2 = "bi-polar"; each item of comparison is examined in some detail separately, usually in its own paragraph, with a minimal introductory or concluding sentence used to name a preference or draw a comparison. (e, f, g)

3 = essentially "bi-polar" in main development, but has at least a paragraph of introduction or conclusion which contains one or more combining sentences establishing a comparison. These papers may also have transitional devices or comparing terms scattered through the "bi-polar" paragraphs. (h, i, j)

4 = "integrated," for the most part, throughout, but unlike Type One, contains some development and some movement from one idea to the next; may be more detailed than Type One, or may relate the entire body of the comparison to other abstract questions such as "how do we choose where to shop?" (k, l, m)

Charles Cooper (1977, 15) reports on the development of the following two scales by four Buffalo-area English teachers—Greg Anderson, Dale

Kaiser, Nathalie Ketterer, and Donald McAndrew. Neither of these scales should be used without reading Cooper's description for each item on the scale (1977, 21–24).

Analytic Scale

Reader _____ Paper _____

	Low		Middle		High
I. General Qualities:					
A. Author's Role	2	4	6	8	10
B. Style or Voice	2	4	6	8	10
C. Central Figure	2	4	6	8	10
D. Background	2	4	6	8	10
E. Sequence	2	4	6	8	10
F. Theme	2	4	6	8	10
II. Diction, Syntax, and Mechanics:					_____
A. Wording	1	2	3	4	5
B. Syntax	1	2	3	4	5
C. Usage	1	2	3	4	5
D. Punctuation	1	2	3	4	5
E. Spelling	1	2	3	4	5

Total _____

Dichotomous Scale

Reader _____ Paper _____

	YES	NO	
I.	_____	_____	Author's role consistent
	_____	_____	Interesting personal voice
	_____	_____	Theme clearly presented
	_____	_____	Background rich and supportive
	_____	_____	Sequence of events clear
	_____	_____	Central figure fully developed
II.	_____	_____	Wording unique and developed
	_____	_____	Syntax correct and varied
	_____	_____	Usage errors few
	_____	_____	Punctuation errors few
	_____	_____	Spelling errors few

Total Yes _____

Patterns of Use

Substantial information is available on the use of various scales. In one school district reading of papers from seventh through twelfth grades, the students in the upper quartile averaged a sum of 22.5 on the Diederich scale above, and students in the lowest quartile averaged 9. On the cohesion scale, the NAEP (1980) reports the percentages in table 1 for seventeen-year-olds at each cohesion level over a ten-year period.

The Gray/Keech scale for a particular comparison topic showed the following distribution among eleventh and ninth graders who had been taught how to write comparisons:

Organizational Rating

	0	1	2	3	4
9th Graders	5.9%	52.9%	29.4%	0	11.8%
11th Graders	0	4.2%	16.7%	16.7%	62.5%

Teachers who use scales are often suspicious of such counts as T-units, but they need numbers for the purpose of reporting to administrators or other teachers what is happening in the classroom. Scales provide numbers and allow for global impressions. Teachers who use analytic scales such as Diederich's should know that Lynn Winters (1979, 25) found that the Diederich scale (DES) and the Winters CSE scale (Current School Education, derived from current composition textbooks) correlate better with General Impression (GI) or holistic scores than they do with T-unit counts (see table 2).

Table 1

Percentages of 17-Year-Olds at Each
Cohesion Score Level, "Stork" Exercise, 1969, 1974, 1979†

Year   *Score Point*

	Non-rateable	Inadequate	Attempts at Cohesion	Cohesion	Cohesion and Coherence	Cohesion or Better
	0	1	2	3	4	3 & 4
1969 (n = 2,073)	1.0%	0.8%	17.8%	67.2%	13.2%	80.4%
1974 (n = 2,281)	1.5	0.6	19.7	64.1	14.1	78.2
1979 (n = 2,748)	0.9	0.6	12.1	70.9	15.5	86.4
Change						
1969–74	0.5	−0.2	1.9	−3.1	0.9	−2.2
1974–79	−0.6	0.0	−7.7*	6.8*	1.4	8.2*
1969–79	−0.1	−0.2	−5.7*	3.7	2.3	6.0*

*Statistically significant at the .05 level.
†Percentages may not total due to rounding error.

Table 2

Intercorrelations among Scoring Systems

System	*Total Sample* n = 80			
	GI	DES	CSE	T-Unit
GI	-			
DES	.82	-		
CSE	.79	.86	-	
T-Unit	.004	.06	.001	-

Descriptive Studies of Texts

Instead of counts and numerical marking of features, some teacher-researchers prefer a descriptive, case-study approach to analyzing texts. The following selection from a study by Ruby Bernstein (Concord High School, Concord, California) and Bernard Tanner (Cubberley High School, Palo Alto, California) illustrates the approach (1977, 15–17):

Paper B (11)   High score—5

I believe physical education should be continued in high school, but in a more progressive system. As it is now many kids shy away from P.E. because of several reasons. One is that the competition is too much. When you have winners, you've got to have losers. Competition is healthy, but I think we place too much importance on being king of the mountain. A more beneficial system would be hiking, or bike riding. Those who want to come in first can do so, but the emphasis should be in bringing out the full athletic potential in each student, instead of those who don't need P.E., they are active enough as it is. Also, by forcing P.E. on kids, you make them reject it that much more. If we had a system by which each student could bring out the good inside we would have a much better attendance record and grade average too.

Paper B (40)   High score—5

I believe physical education should not be required in high school. It accomplishes nothing and is a waste of money.

The only reason I can see for physical education being taught in school is, the school officials believe it keeps the person in shape. This is untrue. If the person doesn't want to participate they won't and nothing can be done to change this. Also, the time alotted for this class is insufficient. The actual time spent in the activity is approximately 30–40 mins. This does nothing for the individual. It is the individual's responsibility to keep their own body shape. If they fail to do this, then *they* must suffer the consequence.

I am not saying physical education shouldn't be taught. I'm just saying it shouldn't be required. It isn't a course that will help you when you leave school. Physical education is just fine as an elective and that's what it should be. If it is made an elective, it just might be fun.

Discussion of B (11) and B (40)

These papers from the top category demonstrate obvious truths—one, that top level papers are by no means perfect; and two, that papers in a given scoring category by no means have a stereotypical sameness.

B (11) consists of a single, fairly well-formed paragraph, beginning with a topic sentence which takes a "clearly defined" and almost unique point of view rather than a mere *pro* or *con* stance, thus at the outset suggesting "complex reasoning." The paragraph supports the point of view with two arguments against the present situation as well as two suggestions for improvements possible in a more "progressive system." The reasoning contains "particular examples" in the matters of "hiking or bike riding," has at least one effective use of diction ("king of the mountain"), and shows some imagination in foreseeing outcomes of better attendance record and grade averages (see concluding sentence). In sum, although the paragraph is somewhat loose in its matters of reference (and even contains one comma-splice), it tends to be reasonably coherent and provides a majority of the key aspects listed for a 5 paper.

B (40) uses the available lined space on the examination paper to offer an answer which has an obvious beginning, middle, and end, with a topic paragraph which takes a specific stand, and a concluding paragraph which has the grace of an effective clincher sentence. The central paragraph contains fairly complex reasoning to explain why the writer believes physical education does not meet the key objective for which (the writer assumes) it is intended, with at least two specific supporting explanations. Overall the paper contains notably effective diction ("accomplishes," "participate," "alotted /*sic*/," "insufficient," "individual," "approximately," "responsibility," "consequences"). Although this paper does show problems with referents (consistency of number in "person/they" and vague-referent "this"), it is otherwise reasonably free of error.

Suggested Studies

1. Does the average level of generality change from grade to grade or from A papers to C papers?

2. Do teacher-readers agree on what is subordinate and what is coordinate in student essays?

3. How do students phrase their main ideas? This question was addressed in a descriptive study by teacher-researcher John A. Higgins (1975).

4. Under what conditions do students increase their uses of parallelism and compare/contrast terms? This question was addressed by teacher-researcher Miki Yamagishi (1980) as part of her research work in the secondary credential program of the Bay Area Writing Project.

5. Do students learn to imitate models? Many teacher-researchers have conducted studies of this question.

4 Cognition:
Information Processing

In Piaget's cognitive perspective, language learning is an interaction between external stimuli and an organism's internal structure. The mechanisms of this interaction are the processes of assimilation and accommodation. In the former, the learner shapes reality to fit internal cognitive structures. In the latter, the learner modifies internal structures to fit the apparent properties of the external stimuli. In such interactions, both the external world and internal cognitive structures can be transformed.

The learner, then, begins with an internal cognitive structure, which in the case of reading and writing can be a mental representation of a text. This mental representation or plan enables the reader or writer to have hypotheses about what might be coming next in that text. Examples of such plans are the five basic types of organization identified by Bonnie Meyer (1982)—comparison, description, response, time-order, and antecedent/consequent. If one predicts what is coming next based on a guess that the text has a time-order plan, then one expects chronology and reads the text as chronology (assimilation) until such time that that guess stops working. Then one modifies the time-order plan (assimilation) or shifts to a completely different plan (accommodation).

In addition to a mental representation of a text or a writing plan, a writer may have a mental representation of cognitive procedures themselves. Theories about cognitive procedures are called metacognition. Three examples of cognitive procedures are (1) the underlining of text for later review, thereby breaking the reading task into two parts, reading itself and review; (2) taking notes while reading, thereby using paraphrasing as an aid to understanding; and (3) putting one's finger on the text as an aid to focusing one's eyes on the correct line. This chapter focuses on both types of mental representation concurrently, first examining the size of the structures being processed and second examining the steps of processing and the relationship between steps and structure.

1 Feature: The Size of the Units Processed

Theory: Cognitive Psychology and Information Processing

Information is processed through two types of memory, short-term and long-term, using two types of memory retrieval, automaticity and attention. Automaticity results when, through practice, processes become consolidated, and memory retrieval becomes automatic. Attention operates as a spotlight on memory, and its memory retrieval is slow.

In all writers, the two mechanisms of memory activation, automaticity and attention, are at work, and can occur simultaneously (Posner and Synder 1975). In the competent writer, the mechanism of automaticity responds to the act of putting letters on a page with two types of analysis. First, there is low-level stimulus analysis of the shape of the letters themselves and of the procedures necessary—holding the pencil, staying on the line. At the same time, automaticity in the competent writer results in high-level semantic analysis of the words and the blocks of meaning associated in memory with the particular words being written. Automaticity is fast, does not use attention, and does not inhibit retrieval. Simultaneously, the mechanism of conscious attention focuses on the mental representations of meaning, activating one as the basis for predictions about what is coming next and inhibiting other information coming from other locations in semantic memory. Attention is slow, has limited capacity, and inhibits the retrieval of information from unexpected locations in semantic memory.

In writers who lack adequate automaticity, a compensatory principle is always at work. When the formation and recognition of words is not automatic, then attention will intervene and take over the function of low-level stimulus analysis (Stanovich 1980). Because attention has limited capacity, the use of attention for low-level stimulus analysis reduces the amount of attention available for high-level semantic analysis. This compensatory principle predicts that students who have difficulty encoding letters automatically will not have adequate attention capacity to integrate large blocks of meaning into a text.

The two mechanisms, automaticity and attention, retrieve information from two types of memory, short-term and long-term. Long-term memory is the storehouse for knowledge about the world and is believed by some to have an unlimited capacity in normal circumstances. Short-term memory is a temporary storehouse for material that is being recognized and attended to, and it has a limited capacity of about seven items, plus or minus two (Miller 1956). Information in short-term memory will decay unless rehearsed. Short-term memory is sometimes called "immediate" or "working" memory, and its limited capacity is called "memory span." The process for increasing the amount of information in short-term memory is called "chunking."

Information-processing theory predicts ways of improving the automatic encoding skills of students, increasing the amount of information that attention can scan in short-term memory, and increasing the length of time that information can be stored in short-term memory. First, practice improves automaticity (LaBerge and Samuels 1974), putting in memory a more efficient copy of procedures for holding the pencil, shaping letters, and so forth. Practice or rehearsal can also increase the length of time that information can be held in short-term memory. In addition, students can be taught various devices for storing information in short-term memory and avoiding the overburdening of short-term memory. Drafts, notes, maps, and other paper records are common devices used for recall.

Second, practice in chunking increases the amount of information that can be held in short-term memory and then analyzed by attention capacity (Miller 1956). Short-term memory has a limit of seven units, but the amount of information in a unit can vary. Chunking is the process of taking several units of meaning (e-t-t-x) and consolidating them into one larger chunk of meaning *(text)*. By changing the seven units in short-term memory from seven letters to seven words, one can increase the amount of information stored in short-term memory. Learning how ideas are connected to one another in a single, meaningful pattern is a common strategy for chunking material into fewer units. In general then, the information-processing system used to write looks something like figure 8.

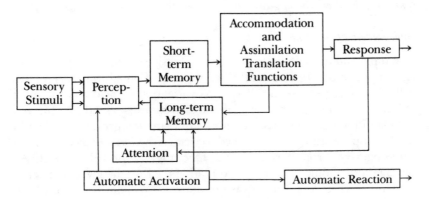

Figure 8. Information-processing system used in writing.

The outline of cognitive theory presented here has its areas of controversy. For one thing, some theorists think that items do not reside in short-term or long-term memory but are at different levels of analysis. They think of the memory system in terms of depth of processing, not storage in a place. Another area of dispute is how to do task analysis—what are the chunks of processing, and what are the parts and the wholes?

Lesson: Fluency

Lessons that focus on fluency are attempting to increase the size of the units that the writer is able to process automatically, thereby releasing attention for organizing larger blocks of meaning. In some school districts, about 20 to 30 percent of the students lack adequate automaticity in low-level stimulus analysis (at the level of letters and words). Lessons to increase fluency or automaticity begin by asking students to write without worrying about "errors" and handwriting, thereby discouraging students from using their attentional capacity for low-level stimulus analysis and encouraging them to leave attention free to attend to purpose and function. "Just get the idea down" and "Think about your story and where it's headed"—these are the teacher remarks that guide attention. The writing in these lessons takes the form of journals, drafts, letters, notes—any form allowing for informality in diction and casual organization. Networking ideas, vocabulary development—these are approaches to chunking.

Making students aware of the processes they use when they write is a new emphasis in many lessons. An example of this approach is the chapter "Understanding Your Own Writing Process" in Linda Flower's 1981 textbook, *Problem-Solving Strategies for Writing*.

Topic and Test Conditions

The topic and test conditions influence the size of the units processed. An emphasis on spelling and other matters of small-unit correctness will, of course, increase the allocation of attention capacity to small units and decrease the attention available for large units. Another topic and test condition variable is the amount of information provided in the test topic. Suppose students were asked to write either on one passage or on three passages from various works. One might expect that the three-passage topic would take longer to read and cause the low-competency students to write less. But this is not the case. William L. Smith (1983) found that topics asking for response to one passage generated far fewer words from low-competency students than did a topic with three passages for comment. Giving more information in the topic apparently helps such students write more.

The analysis of unit size may require, as noted below, a test condition in which students are given the opportunity to make revisions. If the emphasis is on automaticity as reflected in length, then the test conditions might provide a strict limit on the amount of time a student can use.

Coding the Features of Unit Size

Three formulas used to code the size of the units being processed are pauses during writing, the length of the writing sample, and the size of the units that are revised or changed on a second reading. Pause studies are generally not practical for teachers in schools, but several examples are available as models if this approach is desired (Matsuhashi 1981; Myers 1983). The formula for length is a simple count of total words, indicating how much the student was able to process in a given time.

One formula for unit size in revision is suggested by Lillian S. Bridwell (1980). In this formula, the students are given time to review the essays they have written and to make revisions using pens with distinctive colors. These revisions are then coded and counted, using the following categories (1980, 203–4):

1. Surface Level
   1.1 Spelling
   1.2 Punctuation
   1.3 Capitalization
   1.4 Verb form
   1.5 Abbreviations vs. full form
   1.6 Symbols vs. full form
   1.7 Contractions vs. full form
   1.8 Singular vs. plural
   1.9 Morphological conditioning
   1.10 Interlinear and marginal notations related to any of the above
2. Lexical Level
   2.1 Addition
   2.2 Deletion
   2.3 Substitution (synonyms, pronouns)
   2.4 Order shift of single word
   2.5 Interlinear and marginal notations related to single words
3. Phrase Level
   3.1 Addition
   3.2 Deletion
   3.3 Substitution/alteration
   3.4 Order shift of complete phrase

      3.5   Expansion of word to phrase
      3.6   Reduction of phrase to word
      3.7   Interlinear and marginal notations related to phrases
4. Clause Level
   (Subordinate or independent not punctuated as sentence)
      4.1   Addition
      4.2   Deletion
      4.3   Substitution/alteration
      4.4   Order shift of complete clause
      4.5   Expansion of word or phrase to clause
      4.6   Reduction of clause to word or phrase
      4.7   Interlinear and marginal notations related to clauses
5. Sentence Level
   (as punctuated by student)
      5.1   Addition
      5.2   Deletion
      5.3   Substitution/alteration
      5.4   Order shift of complete sentence
      5.5   Expansion of word, phrase, or clause to sentence (includes de-coordination)
      5.6   Reduction of sentence to word, phrase or clause (includes coordination)
      5.7   Transformation
      5.8   Interlinear and marginal notations related to sentence
6. Multi-sentence Level
   (two or more consecutive sentences, categories 6.1–6.5 tallied once for each sentence involved)
      6.1   Addition
      6.2   Deletion
      6.3   Substitution/alteration
      6.4   Order shift of two or more sentences
      6.5   Reduction of two or more sentences to single sentence (excepting those changes accounted for by category 5.6, clause, phrase, or word)
      6.6   Indention
      6.7   De-indention
      6.8   Interlinear and marginal notations related to multiple sentences
7. Text Level (Not included in analysis)
      7.1   Change in function category of essay
      7.2   Change in audience category of essay
      7.3   Change in overall content of the paper
      7.4   Total re-write of essay with few or no one-to-one correspondences between sentences

Patterns of Use

Bridwell found that her twelfth-grade students with low holistic scores, using summary scores from Diederich's scales, made an "overwhelming majority" of their revisions at the surface and word (lexical) levels. The students with high scores, on the other hand, had only a few more total changes but "far fewer surface-level changes." In the substitution of sentences, the high-scoring students substituted far fewer consecutive sentences. In other words, the low-scoring students more often substituted several consecutive sentences in one block. This kind of revision represents the tendency among low-scoring students to start over rather than revise, possibly caused by their failure to give adequate attention to matters of overall organization and purpose.

A second indicator of processing skill is length. Table 3 (Myers 1982, 109) shows the number of words per writing sample of an essay ("explain why someone is a favorite person") and a letter, distributed by score category. The samples were holistically scored by two readers on a 1-to-6 scale, and the two scores added together.

One especially interesting pattern in the data above is the tendency of low writers (group 1) to write more words on letters, whereas all the

Table 3

What Is the Average Number of Words Per Writing Sample in Each Score Category?

1981 Essays

Group	Count	Mean	S.D.	S.E.	95% Conf. Int.
1	38	40.3158	17.85	2.89	34.4483 to 46.1832
2	36	119.8333	38.06	6.34	106.9530 to 132.7137
3	11	149.1818	33.21	10.01	126.8685 to 171.4952
4	26	203.0385	35.96	7.05	188.5124 to 217.5645
TOTAL	111	115.0090	69.61	6.60	101.9149 to 128.1031

1981 Letters

Group	Count	Mean	S.D.	S.E.	95% Conf. Int.
1	23	64.0435	35.41	7.38	48.7289 to 79.3580
2	36	97.1944	22.73	3.78	89.5027 to 104.8862
3	31	122.0323	26.33	4.72	112.3737 to 131.6908
4	12	160.0000	28.57	8.24	141.8422 to 178.1578
TOTAL	102	104.6569	39.99	3.95	96.8020 to 112.5117

other writers wrote more words on essays. One interpretation might be that low writers are more fluent when the audience is more personal, as is the case in the letter. A study of data of this type in a school district might provide a basis for arguing that the district's writing program should give more emphasis to personal writing.

2 Feature: Procedures for Processing

Theory: Metacognition

A writer must use not only information about how texts are organized—comparison, description, and so forth—but also information about how to process information efficiently. These processes or metacognitive procedures have been the focus of a substantial body of research (Emig 1971; Graves 1975) showing that writing is an act of discovery (accommodation) for both skilled and unskilled writers (that is, writers often have only a vague idea of what they are going to write about when they first start); that the writing process is not linear but recursive, moving back and forth across the page; that the writing process often develops in stages, from drafting to finished copy; and that writers appear to pass through developmental stages as they grow as writers.

Lesson: Prewriting and Revising Strategies

In teaching practice, metacognitive theory has led to the introduction of teaching approaches that break the task into parts—note taking or mapping, talking, prewriting, revising—all providing the student with procedures for reducing possible overload on short-term memory. Mapping techniques, for instance, range from actual drawings to clustering and outlines. Talking can take the form of writing groups, collaborative writing in teams or pairs, class discussion, or even the use of a series of questions or heuristics to get ideas flowing or to review what is written (who? what? when? where? why?).

Topic and Test Conditions

The study of metacognitive procedures often requires that students be given enough time to write more than one draft and be provided enough paper so that they can map or prewrite if they choose to. All writing should be submitted and should be coded for the time spent in writing.

The study of writing processes often requires that the sample be restricted to one or two students. Schools almost never do case studies as part of their assessment program, having focused almost entirely on writing *products* as the goal of instruction. However, the study of processes seems particularly appropriate to show the growth and development of young writers and the positive changes in the writing of students who may still be below a school district's standard for minimum competency in writing.

Coding Cognitive Procedures

The formulas for coding cognitive procedures focus on changes in writing procedures from one stage of writing (or draft) to another and on the different procedures used by different writers. One example of a study of procedural changes is Bridwell's study of the kinds of revisions that were made on three different drafts of the same paper. Her formula calculated the total of each type of revision on each draft and then the percentage of each type of revision on each draft.

$$\text{Percentage of each type of revision on a given draft} = \frac{\text{Number of revisions of a particular type on a given draft}}{\text{Total number of revisions on all drafts}}$$

Coding the processes of writing in terms other than revisions is very difficult. Some researchers have tried collecting the prewriting of students and classifying this material into mapping, journals, and so forth. The results do not tell us very much, however, about the development of the students as writers. One problem is that many students prewrite by thinking and not by writing. To capture thinking patterns, scholars have tried four approaches: (1) interviews after the writing episode, inquiring into what students were thinking before and during the writing sample; (2) observation of the writer during the writing process (Graves 1975); (3) videotaping of pauses during the writing episode (Matsuhashi 1979), examining the location and length of these pauses; and (4) audiotaping of students who reflect and compose aloud while they are writing (Emig 1971; Perl 1979; Flower and Hayes 1981). All of these approaches except perhaps for videotaping can be used by most schools. All of these approaches, however, restrict the sample studied to a few cases. In most school situations, one or two students are the limit because case studies generate large amounts of data which require an analysis not easily reducible to a formula and, therefore, not easily understood by those not in the classroom.

The interview approach has the serious drawback of students' not remembering what they were thinking and doing at a particular moment in their writing, and the observation approach has the drawback of requiring the presence of the investigator during the entire writing episode. What Flower and Hayes call *protocol analysis,* using audiotapes, is very practical in most school situations. In Perl's use of this approach, she had the students compose aloud and write with a pen, and the audiotape captured both what the student was saying and the sound of the pen moving across the page. The use of the pen meant that material could be crossed out but not erased. Using the tape and the writing sample, Perl then coded the student's writing behaviors into the following categories (1979, 320–21) (see Perl's report for an example of her coding sheet, using the coding abbreviations listed below):

(1) General planning [PL]—organizing one's thoughts for writing, discussing how one will proceed.
(2) Local planning [PLL]—talking out what idea will come next.
(3) Global planning [PLG]—discussing changes in drafts.
(4) Commenting [C]—sighing, making a comment or judgment about the topic.
(5) Interpreting [I]—rephrasing the topic to get a "handle" on it.
(6) Assessing [A(+); A(−)]—making a judgment about one's writing; may be positive or negative.
(7) Questioning [Q]—asking a question.
(8) Talking leading to writing [T→W]—voicing ideas on the topic, tentatively finding one's way, but not necessarily being committed to or using all one is saying.
(9) Talking and writing at the same time [TW]—composing aloud in such a way that what one is saying is actually being written at the same time.
(10) Repeating [re]—repeating written or unwritten phrases a number of times.
(11) Reading related to the topic:
    (a) Reading the directions [R_D]
    (b) Reading the question [R_Q]
    (c) Reading the statement [R_s]
(12) Reading related to one's own written product:
    (a) Reading one sentence or a few words [R^a]
    (b) Reading a number of sentences together [$R^{a\text{-}b}$]
    (c) Reading the entire draft through [R^{W_1}]
(13) Writing silently [W]
(14) Writing aloud [TW]
(15) Editing [E]
    (a) Adding syntactic markers, words, phrases, or clauses [Eadd]
    (b) Deleting syntactic markers, words, phrases, or clauses [Edel]
    (c) Indicating concern for a grammatical rule [Egr]
    (d) Adding, deleting, or considering the use of punctuation [Epunc]

(e) Considering or changing spelling [Esp]

(f) Changing the sentence structure through embedding, coordination or subordination [Ess]

(g) Indicating concern for appropriate vocabulary (word choice) [Ewc]

(h) Considering or changing verb form [Evc]

(16) Periods of silence [s]

From the codes listed above, Perl was able to get the following information about the student's writing process (322):

(1) the amount of time spent during prewriting;

(2) the strategies used during prewriting;

(3) the amount of time spent writing each sentence;

(4) the behaviors that occur while each sentence is being written;

(5) when sentences are written in groups or "chunks" (fluent writing);

(6) when sentences are written in isolation (choppy or sporadic writing);

(7) the amount of time spent between sentences;

(8) the behaviors that occur between sentences;

(9) when editing occurs (during the writing of sentences, between sentences, in the time between drafts);

(10) the frequency of editing behavior;

(11) the nature of the editing operations; and

(12) where and in what frequency pauses or periods of silence occur in the process.

Flower, Hayes, and Swarts (1980) have given the following advice for those who wish to undertake a study of think-aloud data during the writing process:

1. The hypothesis and then the coding scheme which will be used to analyze thinking-aloud data are developed.

2. The subject works in an experimental room with a desk, writing materials, and a cassette tape recorder and tape.

3. The subject is given a rough idea of the task, and is told, "The most important thing about this experiment is that we want you to say everything out loud as you are thinking and writing your essay, even if it has nothing to do with the task—stray remarks and irrelevant comments are fine. We realize that it is impossible to say everything you're thinking while you're writing, so just try to say as much as you can."

4. The essay and all notes are numbered in chronological order after the subject finishes the writing task.

5. The tape recording is transcribed.

6. Then, using the hypothesis that determined the coding scheme, the transcript is parsed into appropriate units—lines and clauses, processes such as planning and reviewing, or composition episodes.

Patterns of Use

In the Bridwell study (1980), the patterns of revisions (percentages of each type) from one draft to another were as shown in table 4 (1980, 207).

The Perl study focused on unskilled writers involved in both personal reflections on a topic *(reflexive)* and impersonal, objective statements on similar material *(extensive)*. The results in table 5 (1979, 325) on one student show that although the student spent more time prewriting in the extensive mode (7.8/8.0) than in the reflexive mode, the student wrote fewer words. In fact, in session 1, the student wrote more words in the reflexive mode in less writing time (14.5/25.0/24.2 vs. 18.8/51.0).

Sharon Pianko, using videotapes, also did a study of how students divided their time between prewriting and composing. Pianko's sample came from the remedial and traditional (regular) students in a community college. She reported the patterns shown in table 6 (1979, 13).

Descriptive Studies of the Writing Process

Many teacher-researchers will want to attempt studies that are more descriptive of writing in a natural setting. Donald Graves's 1976 study of Michael is such a model of classroom research, which many teachers

Table 4

Percentages of Total Revision Frequencies at Levels and Stages

Level	Stage			Level Percentage
	A	B	C	
Surface	9.00	2.58	13.25	24.83
Word	12.87	5.07	13.30	31.24
Phrase	5.66	3.43	8.91	18.00
Clause	.86	1.22	4.23	6.31
Sentence	1.30	1.63	4.88	7.81
Multiple-sentence	1.16	3.26	7.28	11.80
Stage percentage	30.85	17.29	51.85	

$n = 100; f = 6,129$

Table 5

Tony: Summary of Four Writing Sessions
(Time in Minutes)

			$S1\ TW_1$				$S4\ T \rightarrow W$
		Drafts	*Words*	*Time*	*Drafts*	*Words*	*Time*
Extensive Mode				Prewriting: 7.8			Prewriting: 8.0
		W1	132	18.8	W1	182	29.0
		W2	170	51.0	W2	174	33.9
		Total	302	Total composing: 91.2*	Total	356	Total composing: 82.0*

			$S2\ TW_1$				$S5\ T \rightarrow W$
		Drafts	*Words*	*Time*	*Drafts*	*Words*	*Time*
Reflexive Mode				Prewriting: 3.5			Prewriting: 5.7
		W1	165	14.5	W1	208	24.0
		W2	169	25.0	W2	190	38.3
		W3	178	24.2	W3	152	20.8
		Total	512	Total composing: 76.0	Total	550	Total composing: 96.0

*Total composing includes time spent on editing and rereading, as well as actual writing.

have found helpful in their own projects. Graves began with four classrooms, each with writing folders kept by all the children, and narrowed his focus to Michael. In the classroom, Graves sat next to Michael, observed his every move while writing, and prepared the record shown in table 7 (1975, 232).

Table 6

Factors	Mean Scores		*F-ratio*
	Remedial	Traditional	
1. Prewriting time (minutes)	1.00	1.64	5.2552[a]
2. Composing time (minutes)	35.75	43.29	1.1831
3. Rate of composing (words/minute)	9.31	9.29	0.0001
4. Rereading time (minutes)	3.20	3.71	0.0741

Table 7

Example of a Writing Episode

A whale is eating the	10:12	9-Gets up to get dictionary. Has the page
1 2 3 4 5	R	with pictures of animals.
men. A dinosaur is		
6 7 8 ⑨ ⑩ ⑪ 12	IU	10-Teacher announcement.
triing to eat the whale.	R	11-Copies from dictionary and returns
13 14 15 16 17 ⑱		book to side of room.
A dinosaur is frowning		
⑲ ⑳ ㉑ 22 23 ㉔		18-Stops, rubs eyes.
a tree at the lion. and	RR	19-Rereads from 13 to 19.
㉕ 26 27 28 29 30 31 32	OV	20-Voices as he writes.
the cavman too. the men	OV	21-Still voicing.
33 34 35 ㊱ 37 38	IS	24-Gets up to sharpen pencil and returns.
are killed. The dinosaur		
39 40 41 42 43	RR	25-Rereads from 20 to 25.
killed the whale. The	RR	36-Rereads to 36. Lost starting point.
44 45 46 47 49		
㊽		
cavman live is the roks.		48-Puts away paper, takes out again.
50 51 52 53 54 55 ㊶	RR	56-Rereads outloud from 49 to 56.
	10:20	

KEY: 1-2-3-4—Numerals indicating writing sequence. ④—Item explained in comment column on the right. ////—Erasure or proofreading. T—Teacher involvement; IS—Interruption Solicited; IU—Interruption Unsolicited; RR—Reread; PR—Proofread; DR—Works on drawing; R—Resource use. Accompanying language: OV—Overt; WH—Whispering; F—Forms letters and words; M—Murmuring; S—No overt language visible.

An example of a descriptive study is Jerry Herman's (1979) record of tutoring Brenda in the Laney Community College Writing Center, Oakland, California. The following is a selection from one part of that report (1979, 10):

> Why doesn't the student come up with the correct form the first time? I suspect that students who are inexperienced writers try to write as they speak. For many who speak an American black dialect, "We done our best," would be an adequate spoken form, so Brenda wrote it that way without thinking about its correctness. Inexperienced writers are not accustomed to doing much, if any, proofreading, so the fact that other choices can be made after the initial composing process is nearly irrelevant. The tutor serves as editor (In the "real" world what professional writer doesn't have an editor?), allowing choices to be made and mistakes corrected. This was a revelation to Brenda who—when she did write in school—wrote

something once. Let me correct that: She was asked to re-write things in school but for neatness, not content. To Brenda and who knows how many others, rewriting means nothing more than doing the piece over in your best handwriting—another unconscious deception that many teachers perpetrate on unsuspecting students.

Another example of a teacher's descriptive study of a student's procedures is Miriam Ylvisaker's report on her experiment encouraging fluency. The following is a selection from that report (1979, 7).

> At first Student A would ask only me for help in his proof-reading. He always wrote a rough draft and would bring it to me when everyone else in the class was busy (and unobserving of him) and ask me to point out errors. I underlined, he fixed those he could (on his own or with a dictionary), and then I looked at the paper again and told him where the problem lay with whatever errors he had not been able to correct. Then he wrote a clean draft. This was not a procedure I imposed on him; he initiated it. Later he became freer about asking for help, requesting aid from students as well as from me. "How do you spell it? How does this sound?" he would ask; sometimes he would take the suggestions, but occasionally I heard him say, "No, my way sounds better." Everything he wrote was related in some way or other to sports.

Teachers who, like Ylvisaker, trace classroom processes that contribute to improved writing will often want to quote interactions among students and between teacher and students. The following illustration of this point comes from a classroom study by Deborah D'Amico, who teaches second and third grades in Brookline, Massachusetts (1984, 39–40):

> Ch: This story is boring.
> T: What's boring about it?
> Ch: I don't know. It's just dumb. All I'm doing is listing the people at my birthday party.
> T: Was your party boring?
> Ch: No.
> T: What made it fun?
> Ch: We played some neat games and ate lots of food.
> T: Do you talk about the games in your story?
> Ch: I'm going to, but I still am writing who was there.
> T: Can you think of some other way to write about your party? If this writing is boring, maybe it needs a little excitement added to it. How might you do that?
> Ch: I don't know . . . maybe I could write about something fun that happened . . .

The results of the interaction above can later be traced in the student's writing, showing the impact of talk as a prewriting stage in the writing process. A descriptive approach is particularly useful in studies of the writing of young children, where coding distinctions may be particularly difficult. The following selection from a study by Diane DeFord shows a skillful researcher making a distinction between drawing and writing (1980, 158–59):

> Initially, when a very young child takes pencil (or crayon) to paper and attempts to draw or write, an adult will typically think of it as only scribbling. The child, however, may very well say "That's a pumpkin." At this point, the child's control of the form of written language is not much different from the babbler's control of the form of oral language. "Ba-ba" may be a response to everything said just as scribbling may signify whatever the child intends at the moment (the intent changing from moment to moment as well!). But, when this same child begins to bring subsequent attempts to a parent with the command "Read it to me," the basic function of writing is set. When the child makes the distinction between what is "drawing" and what is "writing," many rules that govern our use of written language rapidly follow.
>
> Kara, for example, at two years of age barely controls the movements required by the task of drawing her family (Figure 2a) and writing her name (Figure 2b).
>
> Bobby, on the other hand, has enough physical control at three years to make his understanding of the basic distinction between drawing and writing very clear (See Figure 3). Physical control aside, both writers show that what they do for writing is different from what they do for drawing . . .

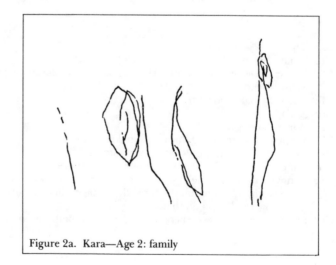

Figure 2a. Kara—Age 2: family

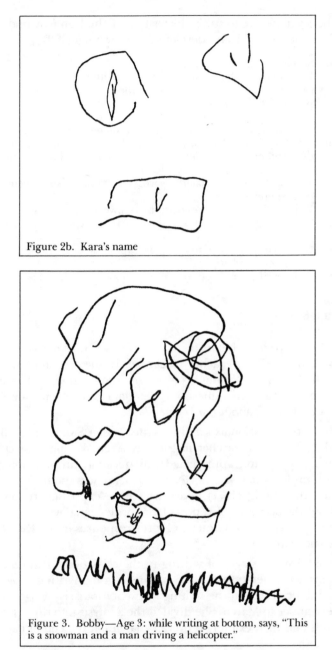

Figure 2b. Kara's name

Figure 3. Bobby—Age 3: while writing at bottom, says, "This is a snowman and a man driving a helicopter."

From "Young Children and Their Writing," *Theory into Practice* 19, no. 3 (1980): 158–59, published by the College of Education, Ohio State University. Reprinted by permission.

Teachers who desire to study the writing of children may find useful DeFord's stages of children's development in writing (162):

1. Scribbling
2. Differentiation between drawing and writing
3. Concepts of linearity, uniformity, inner complexity, symmetry, placement, left-to-right motion, and top-to-bottom directionality
4. Development of letters and letter-like shapes
5. Combination of letters, possibly with spaces, indicating understanding of units (letters, words, sentences), but may not show letter/sound correspondence
6. Writing known isolated words—developing sound/letter correspondence
7. Writing simple sentences with use of invented spellings
8. Combining two or more sentences to express complete thoughts
9. Control of punctuation—periods, capitalization, use of upper and lower case letters
10. Form of discourse—stories, information material, letters, etc.

Suggested Studies

1. How do students begin their planning when they write? Laurie Williams (1979), a teacher-researcher in the credential program of the Bay Area Writing Project, used the methods of Flower and Hayes to study this question. Her data came from one eighth grader writing about *Lord of the Flies*.

2. How do professionals learn to write? Susan Swanson (1983), another teacher-researcher in the Bay Area Writing Project's credential program, approached this question through interviews with professional writers. Teacher-researchers should know, however, that Emig (1971) and others have expressed reservations about the accuracy of reports from professional writers, pointing to the absence of accuracy in Frost's responses in the *Paris Review* as one example.

3. What are the stages of writing in the classroom? Patty Sue Williams, a teacher-researcher from the Virginia Writing Project, examined changes in the writing of twenty-four six-year-olds from September to March. She divided the analysis into three time periods and then examined overall changes at the end of each time period.

5 Social Context

Feature: Relationships among Speaker, Audience, Subject, and Text

Theory: Pragmatics and Frame Semantics

The theory of social context proposes that a piece of writing be understood as a social contract which is shaped by the status, roles, setting, and channel (e.g., typed, printed, handwritten) of the participants in the speech event (Hymes 1974; Brown and Fraser 1979; and Halliday 1978). Bateson (1972) has argued that the social context is like a superordinate message that determines how a given act of communication is to be understood. When the superordinate message is "This is play" in an after-school game, for example, a slap will not necessarily be interpreted as hostile.

Research projects focusing on social context have been influenced first by linguistic theory from pragmatics and frame semantics, both stressing different linguistic roles in typical events (Fillmore 1976; Lakoff 1977); second by work in artificial intelligence showing that social events have set scripts—the restaurant script, for example, including a menu, a waiter/waitress, and so forth (Schank and Abelson 1977); and third by sociolinguistics, particularly the study of the purpose and function of writing in various social settings (Odell and Goswami 1982). In general, the unit of analysis in the study of social context has been at one of four levels: (1) one of the overall purposes of writing (poetic, transactional, reporting, generalizing); (2) particular purposes (personal, logical, concrete, serious, humorous) in specific situations (different roles in a particular business, test responses in different countries); (3) different conventions in different speech events (conversations, lectures, courtroom declarations); and (4) different rules for different speech acts (requests, commands, questions).

For a time, composition textbooks were almost always organized around the modes of writing, but in 1950 James McCrimmon published *Writing with a Purpose,* and since that time purpose and function have become increasingly important as an organizing principle in textbooks and research. Research organized around theories of overall purpose in

89

writing has been heavily influenced by the communication triangle of speaker, listener, and subject. These factors were the basis for work from Aristotle's study of rhetoric (as analyzed in Berlo 1960, 29) to James Moffett's theory of the universe of discourse: "The universe of discourse is staked out by a first person, a second person, and a third person; and their interrelationships make up the dynamics of discourse. So the concept I am referring to is the venerable trinity—I, you, and it; informer, informed, and information; narrator, auditor, and story; transmitter, receiver, and message" (1968, 118).

The components of the communication triangle have been used by different theorists in different ways to define purpose and function. For Moffett, purpose and function are defined by the distances between speaker and subject and between speaker and audience. The distance between speaker and subject ranges from *recording* (I is close to subject which is happening now) and *reporting* (I is slightly removed from subject which happened earlier) to *generalizing* (I is removed from subject enough to give historical overview) and *theorizing* (I is very detached from subject, predicting things that have not happened yet). The distance between speaker and audience, on the other hand, ranges from the close relationships of *reflection* and *conversation* to the detached relationships of *correspondence* and *publication*.

For J. Britton et al. (1975), function categories are based on the speaker/subject relationship, separate from the speaker/audience relationship. There are two writing functions, which originate in a single, basic function, the *expressive*. After the initial development of an idea in the expressive, the writer decides whether to take the additional step of developing the idea as either *poetic* or *transactional* writing. In the poetic function, the writer plays the role of *spectator* to events, but in the transactional the writer plays the role of *participant*. In the former, the writer plays the role of a storyteller of actual and invented events, but in the latter the writer is a doer involved in actual events, someone who is trying to get something done in the world.

Another use of the communication triangle to define purpose is represented by the work of Jakobson, Kinneavy, and Lloyd-Jones, each of whom defined purpose by emphasizing one part of the communication triangle. Roman Jakobson (1960) proposed a communication triangle with six components shaping purpose and function in a communicative event:

CONTEXT
MESSAGE

ADDRESSER -- ADDRESSEE

CONTACT
CODE

Each of these six factors determines a different function of language:

REFERENTIAL

EMOTIVE   POETIC   CONATIVE

PHATIC

METALINGUAL

James Kinneavy (1971) reduced the triangle to four parts—speaker, listener, reality, and signal—and suggested that purpose and language were determined by which of the four parts was being emphasized. If the purpose is to emphasize the speaker, or encoder, then *expressive* language is used. If the emphasis is on the listener, or decoder, then the language is *persuasive;* if on reality or subject, then *referential;* and if on signal, then *literary.*

The National Assessment of Educational Progress (NAEP 1980), under the leadership of its consultants, Richard Lloyd-Jones and Karl Klaus, adopted a theory similar in many respects to that proposed by Kinneavy but restricted to three purposes: *expressive* (emphasizing the addresser), *persuasive* (emphasizing the addressee), and *explanatory* (emphasizing the subject). In effect, NAEP decided that it would not assess literary writing by students in schools.

These uses of the communication triangle in Moffett, Britton, Kinneavy, and the NAEP report all aim for a definition of overall social purpose and function. One problem with much of the data in Moffett, Britton, and others is that all of the writing takes place in one social setting, American or English schools. Purves and others have added additional contexts to these data by examining how school (or test) writing differs among different countries (Takala, Purves, and Buckmaster 1982). In another study, Odell and Goswami (1982) took a somewhat different approach. Instead of looking for an overall purpose in academic writing, they looked for particular purposes embedded in particular circumstances in nonacademic settings. They studied, for instance, the writing of people with different roles and status in a county social service agency. Their findings suggest that although there are context restraints that are of interest, writers, even in nonacademic settings, use some overall principles as guides.

Another approach to the description of purpose in the social context is the speech event approach. This approach differs from the other approaches in that it shifts the emphasis from the analysis of speaker-audience-subject-text as separate dimensions to an analysis of how these relationships co-occur in given speech events. Indeed, J. Britton et al. found a strong association between the expressive function and a very close relationship between speaker and audience (1975, 184). The speech event approach emphasizes the contextual similarities between oral and written language, assuming that the student brings to the writing task the contextual rules learned in speaking.

But what is a speech event and why is this unit of analysis critical? The social contexts of oral language can be divided into three different units of analysis: *speech situations* (football games, meals, fights, ceremonies), *speech events* (conversations, lectures, formal routines), and *speech acts* (commands, declaratives, interrogatives) (Hymes 1974, 51–53). Speech act theorists argue that the meaning of an utterance is determined by its perlocutionary and illocutionary force, not its grammatical features. Thus, "Close the window" is understood as a command not because of matters like subject-verb agreement but because of its habitual speech act functions. Speech act theory, then, is a theory of function and purpose for individual sentences (Austin 1962; Searle 1969), but this framework has sometimes not provided an adequate description of language in social context. Hugh Mehan found in classrooms, for example, many examples of the speech act he called *evaluation*—those individual utterances ("Good," or "That's right") by the teacher in response to some student behavior. He found, however, that a speech act like evaluation could not be adequately understood outside the classroom sequences of initiation-reply-evaluation (1979, 64): "Thus, individual acts of speech are not autonomous. The meaning of a given speech act is not contained within its internal structure. Instead, meaning resides in the reflexive assembly of initiation, reply, and evaluation acts into interactional sequences."

What, then, are the interactional sequences for writing? Myers (1982) suggests that student writing samples are organized around four speech events—*encoding* speech events, *conversations, presentations,* and *rituals*—and that each speech event combines the dimensions of speaker-reader-subject-text into a distinctive set of rules which are, to some degree, recognizable by most students from their oral language experiences.

Theories of purpose and social context are sometimes combined with a developmental perspective. Moffett, in fact, has argued (1967, 117) that the movement from close subjects and audiences to distant ones parallels developmental patterns identified by Piaget:

> The thought and speech of the child, says Piaget, gradually socialize, adapt to a listener. Adapting to a listener is exactly what successful rhetoric entails; the speaker must embrace the other's world by incorporating his point of view and by speaking his language. Thus Piaget enables us to tie rhetoric to the cognitive processes and to the basic biological fact of adaptation in general.

Earlier studies of child language acquisition concentrated on writing "grammars" of child language, but recent acquisition theory has attempted to take into account the effects of context on language learning. The unit of analysis has typically been at two levels, the speech event of language acquisition, called a *joint action format* by Jerome Bruner (1974–75), and *C-acts,* or "protoconversational acts" by John Dore (1979), and the speech acts or individual utterances occurring within the event. Bruner has outlined a developmental sequence of first-year speech acts in child language acquisition: (1) *demand* mode (cries), (2) *request* mode (cries with pauses for response), (3) *exchange* mode (reaching and vocalizing for an object), and (4) *reciprocal* mode, in which mother and child take turns in a common activity and in which the mother provides the scaffolding or support to keep the reciprocal mode going. Speech event theorists in early language acquisition tend to describe C-acts as instances of sharing time, playhouse time, feeding time, and so forth.

In summary, theories of social context have struggled with what the appropriate unit of analysis should be. Four units of analysis common in research on writing and classroom language are: (1) overall purpose and function, (2) different speech situations varying by role, status, and nationality, (3) the speech event, and (4) the speech act.

Lessons: Shifting Relationships among Writer-Reader-Subject-Text

In the design of lessons, Moffet and Britton have been influential in K–12 classrooms. Both have contributed to an interest among educators in a wide variety of writing assignments. Britton found that most classrooms assigned only transactional writing and writing directed to one audience—the teacher—and he recommended that school writing include a variety of different types of audiences and functions. Moffett's 1968 book on the K–12 curriculum introduced many teachers to a rich variety of writing purposes, moving many composition courses away from the limitations of the mode approach.

Topic and Test Conditions

If a writing topic is organized around a particular purpose, then the topic instructions should make that purpose clear. Some topics of the National Assessment of Educational Progress (NAEP) have been criticized for not alerting the writer to the purposes specified in the primary trait scoring guide: for example, Davis, Scriven, and Thomas (1981, 40) point out that "the scoring key for a National Assessment of Educational Progress writing test . . . required the student to write about a color picture of a stag swimming across a river in a burning forest. The key made clear that describing what was there (i.e., doing what was requested) was completely unsatisfactory; one could only get an A by inventing some fanciful background story, something which was not requested."

A second problem in the design of topics and test conditions is the validity of the identified purposes (Davis, Scriven, and Thomas 1981, 38):

> The value of writing for almost everyone lies only in its use for other, usually practical purposes and hence that is the only context in which it can be validly tested. Of course, teachers who believe the contrary will want to test their success in their self-appointed task (e.g., "creative writing"), but such tests are not valid tests of the composition skills that demonstrably need to be learned by all, the basic skill for which the taxpayer pays taxes. Tests of that or those basic skills must relate to their use on a task of independent validity. . . . In the school context there are dozens of such tasks with concurrent validity, e.g., writing up the report on a science project.

Not everyone would agree with Davis, Scriven, and Thomas that storytelling has limited task validity outside of some writing classes. Flower, Hayes, and Swarts have suggested that technical writers use the "scenario principle," a form of narrative or storytelling, in order to "make meaning concrete enough to be *functional* for the reader" (1980, 19). Furthermore, although reports are common in many different subject areas, particular types of reports, such as science projects, may not be taught to all students.

Another problem in topic construction is that a topic attempting to situate a writing task in a school subject matter that all students are assumed to know may be at odds with the writing program in which students have been taught. In an effort to focus only on writing, separate from logic and grammar and other knowledge, many writing teachers promote writing tasks requiring no particular content—"Tell a story," or "Pretend you are a tennis shoe." Thus, many writing classes almost never situate writing in a school subject matter. This tendency can be seen in NAEP's emphasis on expressive purposes and topics over other types— three out of five in the 1979 assessment for seventeen-year-olds.

If primary-trait scoring is to be used, then the topic, topic instructions, and scoring guide should be structured at the same time. The more structured the task, the more reliable the scoring. All scoring systems assume that different writing tasks may have to be judged by different sets of features. In holistic scoring and in Diederich's analytic scale, the features are defined impressionistically by the anchor papers selected from the population of writing samples. In Lloyd-Jones's primary-trait scoring, in addition to anchor papers, the features are defined explicitly by a scoring guide that outlines primary and secondary traits, all organized around a specified identity for the writer and audience and a specified subject matter. In practice, particularly for experienced readers, primary-trait scoring and holistic scoring do not differ very much, perhaps not at all. In both cases, the anchor papers tend to center and stabilize the scoring, providing the definition for the listed trait.

These problems of topic choice are closely related to the question of which unit of analysis is appropriate in a study of social context in writing. Should the topic have a highly generalized purpose, or a specific purpose embedded in a particular subject matter? There are those who argue that "writing for a general purpose" is a school invention, possibly unrelated to the outside world.

Coding and Patterns of Use of Purpose and Social Context

The coding examples that follow have been used by teachers and/or researchers with some valuable results. The first scale is derived from John B. Carroll's study of the scaled responses of 8 expert judges of literature to 150 passages of English prose (Carroll 1960, 285–90). From 68 different dimensions of reader response to literature (Carroll called them qualities of literature), Carroll identified 6 needed to account for all of the ratings of the 8 experts: good-bad, personal-impersonal, ornamented-plain, abstract-concrete, serious-humorous, and characterizing-narrating. Teachers have adapted the Carroll scale (1960, 285–90) for analyzing functions and purposes in student stories and personal narratives which have already been scored. This scale is not to be used for initial scoring. The purpose of the scale is to identify some features of reader response and subject matter, presumably representing some conventions of purpose and function. The teacher can then see how these features interact with scores.

Adapted Carroll Scale

THE PURPOSE: _____

	+3	+2	+1	0 neutral	−1	−2	−3	
GOOD	___	___	___	___	___	___	___	BAD
PERSONAL	___	___	___	___	___	___	___	IMPERSONAL
ORNAMENTED	___	___	___	___	___	___	___	PLAIN
ABSTRACT	___	___	___	___	___	___	___	CONCRETE
SERIOUS	___	___	___	___	___	___	___	HUMOROUS
CHARACTERIZING	___	___	___	___	___	___	___	NARRATING
	+3	+2	+1	0 neutral	−1	−2	−3	

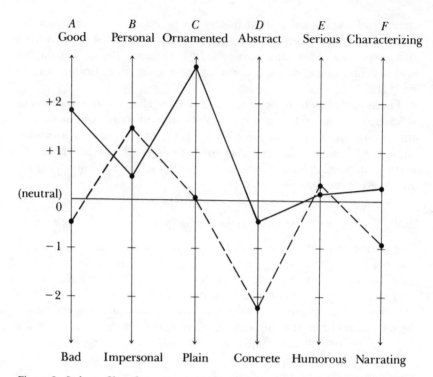

Figure 9. Style profiles of two prose passages: (————) a selection from F. Scott Fitzgerald's *A Diamond as Big as the Ritz;* (– – – –) a selection from Mickey Spillane's *Vengeance Is Mine.*

The results for each dimension should be reported separately. Carroll (1960, 291) reported the results in figure 9 when this scale was applied to short stories by Fitzgerald and Spillane.

A second scale, from the work of Lloyd-Jones (1977), provides for a ranking of primary and secondary traits based on purposes specified in the topic. The scale will often change for each topic. The next two examples of topics and scales come from the National Assessment of Educational Progress. It is recommended that when teachers prepare their own scales, they change the scoring scale so that low numbers reflect inadequate performance and that 0 and 00 be used for uncodable responses.

NAEP's ranking of primary traits is usually on a 1-to-4 scale. Each rank is described by a general feature and sometimes by additional elaboration of the topic. In one expressive topic, students were asked to tell a story about a stork. The scoring of this trait on a 4-point scale ranged from "no evidence of story telling" (1) and "some evidence of story telling" (2) to "clear evidence of story telling" (3) and "structured and complete story telling" (4). The trait itself is based on what is emphasized in topic instructions. For example, in one expressive topic, papers were ranked on how well the writer expressed "feeling through elaboration of a role," the role in this case being one in which the writers were asked to pretend that they were a pair of tennis shoes. Persuasive and explanatory topics have quite different traits. One scale for a persuasive topic ranged from "does not define and defend a point of view" (1) to "does systematically define and defend a point of view" (4).

An example of topic elaboration in the ranking scale is the scale based on the actual subject matter of the writing situation. The scoring focused on the "presence and accuracy of the information given," at one point on the scale giving the writer credit for identifying the account number and mentioning the date and receipt of a collection letter. Many teachers have found that this kind of scale is always necessary for scoring letters because teachers often have quite different notions about which parts are essential and which nonessential to letter form. For example, the argument has been made that the account number expresses audience awareness, enabling the reader to find the writer's account. Others argue that the full name is an adequate expression of the company's identification needs.

A complete example of a scoring guide and its results is shown below. This scoring guide and its results were the follow-up to a topic asking young writers to tell a story about events in a photograph (adapted from Mullis 1975, 18–19, 16):

Scoring Guide: Primary Trait

Categories are listed below.

Entry into World of Picture

- 0 = NO RESPONSE. NO FURTHER SCORING.

- 1 = NO ENTRY INTO THE IMAGINARY WORLD OF THE PICTURE: Respondents write about children, the boat, or about anything else to do with the picture. However, there is only a single statement or the information is too disjointed to make a point: random details, bits of information, or lists of observations that do not create a situation. Also includes pure description, papers that report only what's in the photograph or picture.

- 2 = ENTRY INTO THE IMAGINARY WORLD OF THE PICTURE: Respondents have accepted the world of the picture. However, the control and consistency necessary to create a structured presentation are lacking. Often there is no structure to the world of the picture. This is evidenced by few internal transitions and details that don't harmonize. The ideas may be related, but don't make a whole. Lack of consistency and transitions result in little logical progression of ideas. On the other hand, these papers may have structure, but the narrative is not worked out. There is little imagination on the part of the writer to create the story. An attitude may be stated, but it's not illustrated. You do not "feel" a mood has been created. Other papers may have some structure and the outline of a story or the hint of a mood, yet neither is developed. Generally "2" papers are either undeveloped or developed in a helter-skelter or confusing manner.

3 = GOOD ENTRY INTO THE IMAGINARY WORLD OF THE PICTURE: Papers are generally competent. Respondents evidence the control and consistency to create a structured presentation. Often there are strong topic sentences and good transitions. However, the good quality of the papers is marred by development that is skeletal or somewhat uneven. Narratives display imagination, but often are left with gaps or other unevenness. Details may be inadequate, excessive, or unclear. Attitudes may be stated and somewhat supported, but necessarily presented to "help your friend feel." A definite mood is not created. The underdeveloped paper has a definite beginning and end yet there is not enough material to fill out the structure or it is contrived. The unevenly developed papers either have excessive details or the structure is oddly filled out.

4 = EMOTIVE AND CONSISTENT ENTRY INTO THE IMAGINARY WORLD OF THE PICTURE: These papers are structurally whole. Loose ends have been tied up or cut off (although a strong paper without closure can be rated in this category). Papers are consistent. Narratives are well- and evenly developed or attitudes are expressed so a definite mood is created. You do "feel" the experience. The structure is unified and supported by imaginative and evocative details.

7 = ILLEGIBLE, ILLITERATE. NO FURTHER SCORING.

8 = MISUNDERSTANDS THE TASK OR WRITES ON A TOTALLY DIFFERENT SUBJECT. NO FURTHER SCORING.

9 = I DON'T KNOW. NO FURTHER SCORING.

Fantasy

Story tries to reproduce the fantasy games of children, such as pretending to be pirates, shipwrecked, or riding whales. Stating the fantasy is not enough; two or more unelaborated fantasy situations, or a fantasy situation with at least one elaboration, must be present. Descriptions of games, for example, "follow the leader" or "king of the hill," are not included. Fantasy is more than a literal and logical explanation of the picture.

1 = FANTASY IS PRESENT.

2 = FANTASY IS NOT PRESENT.

Insights
Story develops insights into the writer's perspective on his or her life
or life in general. The message should be integral to the story—not
tacked-on sentiment. The generalizations or social commentaries
can be stated implicitly as well as explicitly. Themes are often based
on positive or negative value statements about childhood or adult-
hood. Reminiscence ("I remember when . . .") is not enough; some
meaningful or intelligent statement must be implied.

1 = INSIGHTS ARE PRESENT.

2 = INSIGHTS ARE NOT PRESENT.

Results

Primary Trait:
Entry into the Imaginary World of the Picture

	1	2	3	4
Age 9	22%	58%	10%	<1%
Age 13	10%	57%	29%	2%
Age 17	10%	35%	44%	10%

	Used Fantasy	Included Insights
Age 9	5%	<1%
Age 13	16%	1%
Age 17	23%	5%

Another example of primary-trait results is the scoring results for the
"principal letter" exercise (NAEP 1980, 32) on page 100, the scoring of
which is shown in table 8. The writing samples were scored on a 4-point
scale, from papers which did not define and defend to the papers which
systematically did.

Table 8

**Percentages of 13-Year-Olds at Each
Primary Trait Score Level, "Principal Letter"
Exercise, 1973, 1978†**

Year	Score Point						
	Non-rate-able	Do Not Define and Defend	Minimal Define and Defend	Define and Defend	System-atic Define and Defend	Margin-al or Better	Compe-tent or Better
	0	1	2	3	4	2, 3 & 4	3 & 4
1973 (n = 2,552)	2.9%	28.0%	40.7%	25.2%	3.2%	69.1%	28.4%
1978 (n = 2,793)	2.3	33.6	43.7	18.5	1.8	64.0	20.3
Change 1973–78	−0.5	5.6*	2.9	−6.7*	−1.4*	−5.1*	−8.1*

*Statistically significant at the .05 level.
†Percentages may not total due to rounding error.

"Principal Letter" Exercise

Imagine that your principal asked for suggestions about how to make things better in your school. Write a letter to your principal telling just ONE thing you think should be changed, how to bring about the change, and how the school will be improved by it. Space is provided below and on the next three pages. Sign your letter "Chris Johnson."

333 West Street
Loden, Ohio 99999
September 5, 1978

Mary Hopkins, Principal
Martin Intermediate School
Loden, Ohio 99999

Another scale combines some of the specificity of primary-trait scoring with parts of the Diederich scale and adds a rating of rater interest. This scale comes from the International Association for the Evaluation of Educational Achievement (1983):

Sample Scoring Sheet
Task 5 — Personal Story

Population _____ Student _____ Rater _____

With Respect to Writer's Choice of Aim and Readership

	Inadequate				Excellent
	1	2	3	4	5

Quality and Scope of Content

1. Thematic appropriateness of what is said ___ ___ ___ ___ ___
2. Presentation of characters, events, and feeling ___ ___ ___ ___ ___

Organization and Presentation of Content

3. Over-all narrative structure ___ ___ ___ ___ ___
4. Appropriateness and control of detail ___ ___ ___ ___ ___

Style and Tone

5. Choice and consistency of tone ___ ___ ___ ___ ___
6. Choice of words and phrases, sentence structures, and larger units of discourse ___ ___ ___ ___ ___

Grammatical features	—	—	—	—	—
Spelling and orthographic conventions	—	—	—	—	—
Handwriting and neatness	—	—	—	—	—

Response of Rater	Low	Medium	High
7. My interest in the composition is	_____	_____	_____
8. My sense of connection with the writer as a person is	_____	_____	_____

Sample Scoring Sheet
Task 6 — Argumentative/Persuasive Composition

Population _____ Student _____ Rater _____

	With Respect to Writer's Choice of Aim and Readership				
	Inadequate				Excellent
	1	2	3	4	5
Quality and Scope of Content	—	—	—	—	—
1. Significance of what is said	—	—	—	—	—
2. Argumentation/Exposition	—	—	—	—	—
Organization and Presentation of Content	—	—	—	—	—
3. Organization of the whole text	—	—	—	—	—
4. Organization of sub-units	—	—	—	—	—
Style and Tone	—	—	—	—	—
5. Choice and consistency of tone	—	—	—	—	—
6. Choice of words and phrases, sentence structures, and larger units of discourse	—	—	—	—	—
Grammatical features	—	—	—	—	—
Spelling and orthographic conventions	—	—	—	—	—
Handwriting and neatness	—	—	—	—	—

Response of Rater	Low	Medium	High
7. My interest in the composition is	_____	_____	_____
8. My sense of being persuaded by the composition	_____	_____	_____

A quite different index of social context attempts to estimate the degree to which various words and phrases in the writing sample are signaling particular social relationships between writer and audience (distancing), writer and subject (processing), and writer and text (modeling). *Conversational* distancing is close, and *presentational* far; conversational processing projects an approximate world, presentational a normative and hierarchical world; and conversational modeling indicates a transitory text, presentational a permanent text. The formula and some results (adapted from Myers 1982, 66–67, 140, 135) are shown below and in tables 9 and 10. See Myers (1982) for other examples of words and phrases indexing particular relationships.

Speech Event Scale

Conversational Distancing (Close Distancing):

$$\frac{\text{You (us, ours)} + \text{me (my, mine)} + I \text{ comments (I think, I believe)}}{\text{Total Words}} + \begin{array}{c}\text{One-time orientations}\\ \text{(I am writing about)}\end{array}$$

Presentational Distancing (Far Distancing):

$$\frac{\text{Distant sentence subjects (nouns)} + \text{new information marker (A)}}{\text{Total Words}} + \begin{array}{c}\text{Opening sentence without}\\ \text{I, me, my, you in}\\ \text{subject position}\end{array}$$

Conversational Processing (Approximate Processing):

$$\frac{\text{and, (but, or)} + \text{hedges (sorta)} + \text{leaps (really, a lot)}}{\text{Total Words}}$$

Presentational Processing (Normative and Embedded Processing):

$$\frac{\text{embeddings (if, who, however)} + \text{-ing modifiers} + \text{qualifications (in general, perhaps)}}{\text{Total Words}}$$

Conversational Modeling (Transitory Modeling):

$$\frac{\text{Punctuation Mark (!, CAPS, underlining)} + I + \text{slang (gotcha)}}{\text{Total Words}} + \begin{array}{c}\text{One-time ending}\\ \text{(The End)}\end{array}$$

Presentational Modeling (Permanent Modeling):

$$\text{Title} + \text{a statement marked as a conclusion at the end}$$

Table 9

Analysis of Presentational Markers in Essays from 1980 to 1981

Combined					
1 (low)	44	1.4558	.7602	.1146	1.2247 to 1.6869
2	78	3.3831	2.5855	.2927	2.8001 to 3.9660
3	65	3.9951	1.8188	.2256	3.5445 to 4.4458
4 (high)	40	8.2515	4.3343	.6853	6.8653 to 9.6377
TOTAL	227	4.0426	3.3399	.2217	3.6058 to 4.4794

In the combined data for essays, the following pairs of groups show significant differences in the frequency of presentational markers: 1-2, 1-3, 1-4, 2-4, and 3-4 (at the $p < .05$ level or beyond).

Table 10

Analysis of Conversational Markers in Essays
from 1980 and 1981

Combined					
Group 1	44	.5073	.5582	.0842	.3376 to .6770
Group 2	78	*.5166	.9486	.1074	.3027 to .7305
Group 3	65	.3182	.3672	.0455	.2272 to .4092
Group 4	40	*.1534	.1786	.0282	.0963 to .2105
TOTAL	227	.3940	.6551	.0435	.3083 to .4797

*Group 1 = Low; Group 4 = High
*The two groups showing a significant difference in the combined essays are groups 2 and 4 (at the p < .05 level or beyond).

Because the study of social context is still relatively new and research approaches vary widely, few trends in student practices can be reported. However, one interesting pattern is the variation of different countries on the scale of Takala, Purves, and Buckmaster (1982, 119):

Factor

Country	Personal	Ornamental	Abstract	Single	Logical
Australia	High	High	Low	High	Low
England	Medium	Low	Low	Low	Low
Federal Republic of Germany	High	Low	Low	Low	Low
Finland	Low	Low	Low	Low	Low
Israel	High	Medium	Low	High	High
Italy	High	High	High	High	High
Ivory Coast	Medium	Low	Low	Low	Low
Japan	High	Low	High	High	Medium
Netherlands	High	Low	Low	Low	Low
New Zealand	Low	Low	Medium	Low	Low
Nigeria	Low	Low	Low	Low	Low
Scotland	Low	Low	Low	Low	Low
Thailand	High	High	Medium	Medium	Low
United States	Low	Low	Low	Medium	High

Suggested Studies

1. Can the social context of the writing class be altered so as to improve writing? To approach this question, the teacher-researcher needs some assumptions about what "improve" means and a hypothesis about how to alter the class. Miriam Ylvisaker (1979), a

teacher-researcher from the Bay Area Writing Project, approached this question with the assumption that "improvement" meant increased fluency, or more writing, and with the hypothesis that her high school class in Oakland, California, could be altered to provide for more peer response to student writing. Joan Duvall-Flynn, a teacher-researcher from West Chester, Pennsylvania, approached this question with the assumption that "improvement" meant such things as "more story words" and "better structuring of events" and with the hypothesis that a fifth-grade class could be altered to provide a productive setting for four boys who were behind.

2. Melissa Davison (1979), a teacher-researcher from the credential program of the Bay Area Writing Project, decided to examine the influence of social context on student writing by studying how changing the audience changed the language the students used in their writing.

6 Other Approaches

Other approaches to studying student writing and writing classes include the examination of (1) the teaching of the conventions of standard English, as reflected in the "errors" in the writing samples; (2) student attitudes toward writing and various teaching approaches; and (3) the variety of approaches to the teaching of writing. All three features have persistent and serious problems of coding and interpretation. Nevertheless, school districts in their assessments often focus on one or more of these features.

1 Feature: "Errors"

Theory: Errors and Expectations

There are those who still insist that a concern about errors in school writing is the result of one social class's trying to exploit another. Among those concerned about errors in school writing, however, the general view is that language is a habitual code, not necessarily a logical one, and that students who do not have control over the dominant code face serious communication difficulties when they venture into the world of colleges and commerce (Shaughnessy 1977).

The study of errors in writing has undergone a radical change in its theoretical assumptions during the last twenty years, especially because of a growing interest of the public schools in educating students who had formerly been pushed out or kept out. As part of the War on Poverty in the 1960s, the dropout from secondary classrooms became a problem for the schools to solve rather than a status symbol, and at the same time public colleges and universities began attempting to educate the students entering under new open-admissions policies. The change in theoretical assumptions was reflected in the names given the courses for students with many errors in their writing. These new courses were at first called "bonehead" English, then "remedial" English, and later "English for the disadvantaged." The current term is "basic writing" (Bartholomae 1980; Shaughnessy 1976).

Some of the present assumptions about "errors" are that written language is in many ways a second language, requiring for its teaching some of the techniques of foreign language instruction (Allen 1970); that well-educated adults have at least three "dialects" available to them for writing—unplanned, planned for narratives and descriptions, and planned for exposition (Krashen 1978); and that students who are not so well educated have *basic writing,* a type of writing which these writers use as an occasion to acquire or learn the other types or "dialects" of writing. Basic writing, then, represents stages of acquisition or learning, not failure or arrested development (Bartholomae 1980).

In the second-language model, natural acquisition and learning are the two ways that adults internalize the rules for a second language, according to Krashen's monitor model (1978). Acquisition is the natural way, similar to language acquisition among children, and results in a feel for the "correctness" of acquired rules. Learning is the internalization of rules through conscious knowledge and results in knowing a few rules. Acquisition is far more important to the language user. It is the acquired language system that has most of the rules embedded in a feel for "correctness" and that initiates the sentence. The learned language system can only operate on the output of the acquired system and can only store the simplest rules—"It is difficult to carry complex rules around as mental baggage," says Krashen (1978, 176). The learned language system, then, acts as a monitor that students can use on what they have already written. Some students do everything by feel, having no use for the monitor system, and others are monitor overusers, reluctant to speak unless they know the rule (Krashen 1978).

The question of how to reduce errors in student writing is a complicated matter. First, the reduction of the incidence of an error may have negative effects on other aspects of a student's writing. For instance, the reduction of spelling mistakes may reduce fluency among writers who need to develop smooth motor routines in writing. Second, some errors are an indication of new improvements in writing development and should not be reduced prematurely. For instance, errors in modification and nominalization can occur when students start to write more on academic subjects. Teacher attention to these errors could force students to return to easier topics in order to protect themselves from criticism.

Finally, errors may have different conceptual foundations rather than a common foundation. Shaughnessy (1977) has suggested that four grammatical concepts underlie most student misunderstandings about form: (1) the sentence, particularly the base words of subject and predicate; (2) inflection, particularly the way the concept works in different languages; (3) tense, recognizing that the point is to teach a verb system, not the experiential concept of time; and (4) agreement. Shaughnessy uses many different devices for teaching these concepts, including sentence combining, the development of analogies, and focused drill.

The teaching of rules alone seems to achieve limited results in the reduction of error. Sherwin reports, "It appears that rules offer limited help in the teaching of spelling" (1969, 106), and Elley et al. report that the direct effects of the study of transformational grammar on the language growth of secondary school pupils are "negligible" (1976).

The grammar program in the Elley study explained phrase structure and transformational rules, and at the end of the course 94 percent of the students were largely correct in their analysis of sentences. After two years of study, however, no differences appeared among students in the grammar program and two other programs. After three years, the students in the grammar program showed "small differences . . . in some minor conventions of usage" (Elley et al. 1976, 18). In his review of the literature, Sherwin came to a similar conclusion: "After a tally of procedural and other limitations, the research still overwhelmingly supports the contention that instruction in formal grammar is an ineffective and inefficient way to help students achieve proficiency in writing" (1969, 168).

Lessons: Usage, Punctuation, Capitalization, and Other Conventions

From David Holbrook (1961) to Mina Shaughnessy (1977), a number of excellent teachers have given many useful examples of lessons which have worked with basic-writing students, that is, inspired the acquisition of greater proficiency. Most of these approaches emphasize situations in which rule-learning is a secondary, not a primary, focus.

Topic and Test Conditions

Some topics and some conditions produce more errors in writing, the results varying not only by differences in students but by differences in the errors targeted for study. Another issue is whether the errors are to be divided into perceptual errors and other types. Perceptual errors are "slips-of-the-eye" which are corrected when the student rereads the paper. If these errors are to be eliminated from the study, then time must be provided for students to reread papers. The method of rereading can also make a difference. Some students seem to perceive some errors only when they read the errors aloud.

Coding of Errors

The errors that should be coded are those which make a difference to teachers. Some errors are associated with second-language and dialect interference. For example, the following errors are among those associated with a student using Spanish phonology in the writing of English (Moore and Marzano 1979, 161):

1. Improper word order in main clause
2. Improper pronoun (e.g. *he* for *you*)
3. Adjective used as noun
4. *s* ending on an adjective
5. Improper agreement
6. Omitted *s* for possessive form of noun
7. Improper formation of irregular possessive pronoun (e.g. *you* for *your*)
8. Improper word order with adverbs modifying verbs
9. No auxiliary with negative and interrogation
10. Use of present for past
11. Use of present for present perfect
12. Use of past for present
13. Improper formation of past participle
14. Contractions not fully developed (e.g. *don* for *don't*)
15. Improper present participle ("I am ready for to read" for "I am ready for reading")
16. Improper subject/verb concord of number
17. Subject/verb word order reversed
18. Third person subject not stated
19. Double subject (The teacher, he is late)
20. Omitted coordinate conjunction
21. Omitted preposition (I live Main Street)

The following are examples of spellings which have been identified as associated with black dialect (Groff 1978, 23):

Standard spelling—*Dialect related spelling*

1.	side	— *sie, site*	13.	hold	— *hode, hole*
2.	rub	— *ruh, rup*	14.	hard	— *hod, har*
3.	flat	— *flah, flad*	15.	warm	— *warn*
4.	cross	— *craw*	16.	melt	— *met*
5.	size	— *sie, sice*	17.	fix	— *fisk, fis*
6.	jar	— *jah*	18.	these	— *dese*
7.	bell	— *beh*	19.	three	— *thee, tree*
8.	game	— *gae, gane*	20.	ten	— *tin, tem*
9.	reading	— *readin*	21.	best	— *bist*
10.	mouth	— *mouf, mout*	22.	chair	— *cheer*
11.	fast	— *fas, fah*	23.	poor	— *pore*
12.	plant	— *plat, plan*	24.	still	— *steel*

And the following spelling problems have been associated with developing orthographic concepts in young children (Beers and Henderson 1977, 137):

Spelling Pattern Sequences

Category	*Examples*
Short vowels	
Short *a* as in *cat*	
1. omission of *a*	CT *(cat)*, LT *(last)*, HVE *(having)*, SIP *(slap)*, MTR *(matter)*
2. *e* substituted for *a*	THET *(that)*, KREB *(crab)*, EM *(am)*, HED *(hand)*, HEPED *(happened)*, CEM *(can)*
3. correct form begins to appear	
Short *e* as in *met*	
1. *a* substituted for *e*	WAN *(when)*, WAT *(went)*, GAT *(get)*, CAP *(kept)*, FALT *(felt)*, STAPT *(stepped)*, DRAS *(dress)*
2. *i* substituted for *e*	WINT *(went)*, SLIDEG *(sledding)*, MODL *(metal)*, KIDL *(kettle)*
3. correct form	
Short *i* as in *hit*	
1. *e* substituted for *i*	MES *(miss)*, HEZ *(his)*, DEFRET *(different)*, SCEN *(skin)*, LEST *(list)*, CHECKS *(chicks)*
2. correct form	
Short *o* as in *stop*	
1. *i* substituted for *o*	GITN *(gotten)*, TIP *(top)*, GRASHIPR *(grasshopper)*
2. *u* substituted for *o*	STUPIG *(stopping)*, SLUPE *(sloppy)*, GRASHUPIR *(grasshopper)*
3. occasionally correct form	
Short *u* as in *up*	
1. *i* appears for *u*	JIMPING *(jumping)*, BINE *(bunny)*, INTILL *(until)*, PITE *(putty)*
2. *o* for *u*	THODER *(thunder)*, CROSHD *(crushed)*, SNOGOUL *(snuggle)*, SNOK *(snuck)*
3. *a* appears for *u*	SADN *(sudden)*, CRASHER *(crusher)*, FANE *(funny)*
ou as in *would*	
1. *u* for *ou*	SUD *(should)*
2. occasionally correct	

The following is the list of errors developed by the National Assessment of Educational Progress in its study of errors in papers by seventeen-year-olds:

I. Sentence Level Mechanics Categories
    A. Sentence Types with Punctuation Errors (sentences that do not fall into any of the syntax categories).
        1. *Run-on Sentence*
            a. Fused—A sentence containing two or more independent clauses with no punctuation or conjunction separating them.
            b. On and on—A sentence consisting of four or more independent clauses strung together with conjunctions.
            c. Comma splice—A sentence containing two or more independent clauses separated by a comma instead of a semicolon or a coordinating conjunction.
        2. *Incorrect Fragment*—A word group, other than an independent clause, written and punctuated as a sentence.
    NOTE: The scoring of T-unit constituents made it possible for some of the preceding sentence types to be derived through data analysis for the "Rainy Day" papers.
    B. Faulty Sentence Construction (These scores are in addition to the sentence types.)
        1. *Agreement Error*—A sentence where at least one of the following is present: subject/verb do not agree, pronoun/antecedent do not agree, noun/modifier do not agree, subject/object pronoun misused, and/or verb tense shifts.
        2. *Awkward Sentence* (The awkward categories are listed in order of category precedence, since only one score was given to a sentence.)
            a. Faulty parallelism—A parallel construction that is semantically or structurally dysfunctional.
            b. Unclear pronoun reference—A pronoun's antecedent is unclear.
            c. Illogical construction—Faulty modification or a dangling modifier or a functionally misarranged or misproportioned sentence.
            d. Other dysfunctions—A sentence containing an omitted or extra word and/or a split construction that definitely detracts from readability.
II. Punctuation Errors—Every error of commission and error of omission is scored for commas, dashes, quotation marks, semicolons, apostrophes, and end marks. The most informal rules of usage are used with the writer receiving the benefit of any doubt.
III. Word-Level Mechanics Categories
    A. Word Choice—The writer needs a word that is different from the one written. This category also includes attempts at a verb, adjective, or adverb form that is nonexistent or unacceptable.
    B. Spelling—In addition to a misspelling, this category includes word division errors at the end of a line, two words written as one,

one word written as two, superfluous plurals, and groups of distinguishable letters that do not make a legitimate word.

C. Capitalization—A word is given a capitalization error score if the first word in a sentence is not capitalized, if a proper noun or adjective within a sentence is not capitalized, and if the pronoun "I" is not capitalized.

Patterns of Use

After the coding and error counts are completed, the investigator must decide what the baseline will be in order to report results. Table 11 (adapted from NAEP 1980, 46) uses a combination of percentages (What percentage of all sentences in the group were fragments?) and numbers (What was the average number of capitalization errors on papers in the group?). The mean is the average for all groups of seventeen-year-olds in the national sample, the median is the point which 50 percent of the students are above and 50 percent below, the first quartile represents the point which 25 percent of the students were above and 75 percent below, the third quartile represents the point which 75 percent of the students are above and 25 percent below, and the 90th percentile represents the 10 percent of the students who are the most error-prone. Notice that the patterns of error vary from one kind of writing to another.

2 Feature: Student Attitudes

Theory: Personality Studies

One of the ways that teaching practices are assessed is an examination of the responses of the students. One theoretical framework in which such assessments are done is provided by the work of Carl Rogers (1951) and Abraham Maslow (1954). For Rogers, successful teaching enables students to become congruent personalities. The total personality has two domains, one of self-structure and the other of experience. When self-structure includes surrounding experience, the personality is congruent. For example, if a student regards the writing assignments in a writing class as threatening and demeaning, then the writing class is not facilitating the student's development as a congruent personality.

For Maslow, development into a congruent personality occurs in stages, each stage focused on salient needs and each stage leading to a higher level of human motivation. The first stage begins with basic physiological needs such as food and drink and leads to a need for security, order, and protection in the second stage. In the third stage, the salient

Table 11

Means and Percentiles for Errors in Narrative and Descriptive Papers, Age 17, 1969, 1974, 1979†

	1969					1974					1979				
	Mean	Q1	Median	Q3	90th	Mean	Q1	Median	Q3	90th	Mean	Q1	Median	Q3	90th
Narrative ("Stork")															
% sentence fragments	1	0	0	0	0	2	0	0	0	9	2	0	0	0	8
% run-on sentences	3	0	0	0	17	6	0	0	6	20	5	0	0	6	17
% awkward sentences	14	0	12	25	40	15	0	11	25	40	15	0	11	23	40
# capitalization errors	1	0	0	1	2	1	0	0	1	2	1	0	0	1	2
% misspelled words	2	0	1	3	5	2	1	2	4	6	2	1	2	3	6
% word-choice errors	1	0	0	1	2	1	0	0	0	3	1	0	0	1	2
% sentences with agreement errors	2	0	0	0	9	3	0	0	0	11	2	0	0	0	11
# total punctuation errors	6	2	4	8	13	6	2	5	8	15	6	3	5	8	13
Number of respondents			365					417					538		
Descriptive ("Describe")															
% sentence fragments	4	0	0	0	14	5	0	0	6	20	4	0	0	0	14
% run-on sentences	7	0	0	10	25	10	0	0	11	38	7	0	0	12	33
% awkward sentences	16	0	11	25	43	18	0	13	25	43	19	0	15	29	50
# capitalization errors	0	0	0	1	1	1	0	0	1	2	1	1	0	1	2
% misspelled words	3	1	2	3	6	3	1	2	4	7	3	0	2	5	8
% word-choice errors	1	0	0	1	2	1	0	0	0	2	1	0	0	1	2
% sentences with agreement errors	7	0	0	11	25	9	0	0	12	29	8	0	0	13	25
% total punctuation errors	2	1	2	4	5	3	1	2	4	6	3	1	3	4	7
Number of respondents			365					417					538		

†*Statistically significant at the .05 level.*
Figures for means and percentiles have been rounded to the nearest whole number.

need is social, a desire for "belongingness," and in the fourth stage the need is for self-esteem, prestige, and status. Finally, in the fifth stage, human beings become self-actualizing. Maslow studied self-actualizing persons in history and contemporary society and found that they were more efficient in perceiving reality, more accepting of themselves, more spontaneous, more able to center on problems and their solutions, and more able to resolve moral dichotomies and their dilemmas. For Maslow, a successful writing class would contribute toward student growth through this hierarchy of motivations. For writing researchers, the issue becomes the study of the effects of writing apprehension on students and possible treatments for anxious students (Daly and Miller 1975, 248).

Lessons: Increasing Self-Esteem and Facilitating Personality Growth

A number of teachers have used the theories of Maslow and Rogers in the design of lessons for the classroom. Several examples can be found in *Building Self-Esteem through the Writing Process* by Lynn Howgate and in *If Maslow Taught Writing* by Ada Hill and Beth Boone. Hill and Boone provide examples of ways to help students at different levels in Maslow's hierarchy.

Topic and Test Conditions

If questionnaires are used, then students must be encouraged to give accurate and complete responses. Without encouragement, students tend toward incomplete and inaccurate responses.

Coding and Patterns of Use

Hill and Boone have suggested giving students the two scales on pages 114 and 115 (1982, 17–18) and having students place X's over the five "gripes" and "why-writes" that most closely express their attitudes.

Hill and Boone have arranged these scales to represent different levels in Maslow's hierarchy of growth. For gripes, they used the following scoring (1982, 16–19):

> The diagonal row of boxes from the upper left corner to the lower right corner (numbers 1, 7, 13, 19, and 25) are responses that indicate a strong need for belonging, sharing, and peer support.
> The triangle to the left of that diagonal contains both basic and safety level gripes (basic-numbers 6, 12, 18, 22, and 24; safety numbers 11, 16, 17, 21, and 23).
> The triangle on the right of the diagonal has complaints vocalized as a result of the need for ego reward and the need to self-actualize (ego-numbers 2, 4, 8, 14, and 21; self-actualization-numbers 3, 5, 9, 10, and 15).

Writing Gripes

1. If I'm going to write, it has to be something that will be read and answered, like a note or a letter.

2. Writing makes me feel bad. I put lots of work into a paper and all I get is a grade.

3. I wouldn't mind writing if I got to write the things I want to write.

4. It's dumb to write for a class. Real writing, for a newspaper or a magazine, would be better.

5. Why should I write only what my teacher tells me to write? I want to create a story or a poem.

6. I never have paper or a pen. If teachers want me to write, they must give me the things I need.

7. If we could work in groups and write together, I'd like to write. I don't like to sit by myself and write.

8. The thing that makes me mad is I have to write and no one sees it except my teacher. I want others to see what I can do.

9. I like to write when I choose to, but I hate to write at school or on school assignments.

10. I like to write. In fact, I get so involved that I am lost in my writing, but at school, I'm not allowed to get that involved.

11. I don't like to write because no one will help me start.

12. How can anyone be expected to write in a classroom? It's dirty, noisy, and crowded.

13. Writing for a teacher is stupid. I want to share my ideas and writing with my friends.

14. I'd write more but no one appreciates it. I'd rather spend my time doing something worthwhile.

15. Teachers are so unfair. They only accept writing they like and agree with.

16. They tell me to use a dictionary and a grammar book, but I'm not able to find the right word or page.

17. I can't spell or punctuate. It would be better if I learned that first, then I could write.

18. Teachers want me to use a dictionary. If I had one, I'd use it. Why aren't there enough here?

19. I don't like to write by myself. I need to be with a group of people before I can do my best.

20. Writing is useless. I need to spend my time doing something that lets people really notice me.

21. I can't write if I don't know what to do. A teacher should show me how!

22. Teachers say they can't read my handwriting. It is silly to write if no one can read it.

23. I hate being told to write a composition about anything I choose. I want good directions and a good assignment.

24. I can't write because I'm always too tired or hungry.

25. I get mad when I have to be quiet. How can I write if I can't share my ideas with a friend first?

Why Write?

1. To record announcements and minutes for a club or group you belong to.	2. To enter writing contests.	3. To help you make decisions about what you have read or heard.	4. To develop yourself as the kind of writer that you want to be.	5. To help you find happiness expressing your thoughts.
6. To do as well as your friends do in school.	7. To express your opinions, such as in a letter to an editor, teacher, or principal.	8. To give effective speeches.	9. To keep track of your thoughts and feelings in a diary or journal.	10. To improve your own writing style.
11. To pass written assignments given in class.	12. To work with others on group projects and reports.	13. To correspond with your family or friends to tell them what is happening to you.	14. To present your views to others to convince them that you are right.	15. To experiment with new ways of expressing your ideas.
16. To describe something, such as a party or an accident.	17. To copy your favorite song lyrics, poems, sayings, etc.	18. To explain to someone how to do or make something.	19. To show that you can do better work than others in your class.	20. To see your name and works in print.
21. To take a message for someone.	22. To fill out forms.	23. To give directions on how to get from one place to another.	24. To help someone else with a problem.	25. To entertain other people.

For why-write, they used the following scoring (1982, 19):

> The boxes in the lower left-hand corner (numbers 11, 16, 17, 21, 22, and 23) represent the safety-level students' perceptions of the reasons for school-related writing. Students on the belonging-level most frequently respond to boxes 1, 6, 12, 18, 24, and 25. On the other hand, ego need–level students tend to mark boxes numbered 2, 7, 8, 14, 19, and 20, and students on the self-actualizing-level most frequently respond to those numbered 3, 4, 5, 9, 10, and 15. The center box, number 13, could be labelled "free," since it is the one most often chosen by all level students. Notice that none of the boxes is normally chosen by students with truly basic needs. Basic-need students usually see no reason for writing at all.

Both Hill and Boone provide numerous cautions about using such scales to diagnose individual student needs. However, they believe that such scales do provide interesting clues about some of the attitudes developing in a writing class.

Daly and Miller (1975, 245–46) report that the following scale has proven to be a reliable instrument for measuring writing apprehension (+ indicates writing apprehension; drop + and − when scale is used with students):

> Directions: Below are a series of statements about writing. There are no right or wrong answers to these statements. Please indicate the degree to which each statement applies to you by circling whether you (1) strongly agree, (2) agree, (3) are uncertain, (4) disagree, or (5) strongly disagree with the statement. While some of these statements may seem repetitious, take your time and try to be as honest as possible. Thank you for your cooperation in this matter.
>
> (+)   1. I avoid writing
> (−)   2. I have no fear of my writing being evaluated
> (−)   3. I look forward to writing down my ideas
> (+)   4. I am afraid of writing essays when I know they will be evaluated
> (+)   5. Taking a composition course is a very frightening experience
> (−)   6. Handing in a composition makes me feel good
> (+)   7. My mind seems to go blank when I start to work on a composition
> (+)   8. Expressing ideas through writing seems to be a waste of time
> (−)   9. I would enjoy submitting my writing to magazines for evaluation and publication
> (−) 10. I like to write my ideas down
> (−) 11. I feel confident in my ability to clearly express my ideas in writing
> (−) 12. I like to have my friends read what I have written
> (+) 13. I'm nervous about writing

(−) 14. People seem to enjoy what I write
(−) 15. I enjoy writing
(+) 16. I never seem to be able to clearly write down my ideas
(−) 17. Writing is a lot of fun
(+) 18. I expect to do poorly in composition classes even before I enter them
(−) 19. I like seeing my thoughts on paper
(−) 20. Discussing my writing with others is an enjoyable experience
(+) 21. I have a terrible time organizing my ideas in a composition course
(+) 22. When I hand in a composition I know I'm going to do poorly
(−) 23. It's easy for me to write good compositions
(+) 24. I don't think I write as well as most other people
(+) 25. I don't like my compositions to be evaluated
(+) 26. I'm no good at writing

Another instrument used to measure student attitudes is the student questionnaire used by the National Assessment of Educational Progress, shown in table 12.

Table 12

National Percentages of Responses to Attitude Questions about Writing, Age 13, 1978

On this and on the next page are statements about writing. There are no right or wrong answers to these statements. Please indicate how much you agree or disagree with each statement by filling in the oval under the appropriate response. While some of the statements may seem repetitious, take your time and try to be honest as possible.

	Strongly Agree	Agree	Uncertain	Disagree	Strongly Disagree
A. I like to write down my ideas.	12.9	44.3	21.8	16.2	4.7
		57.2		20.9	
B. I am no good at writing.	7.5	16.8	21.7	37.8	15.9
		24.4		53.7	
C. Expressing ideas through writing seems to be a waste of time.	6.3	11.9	16.3	39.9	25.3
		18.3		65.1	

	Strongly Agree	Agree	Uncertain	Disagree	Strongly Disagree
D. People seem to enjoy what I write.	6.5	21.1	47.5	15.5	9.3
		27.6		24.8	
E. I expect to do poorly in composition classes before I take them.	4.7	12.4	20.8	41.1	20.7
		17.1		61.9	
F. I look forward to writing down my ideas.	10.3	33.6	22.5	23.7	9.7
		43.9		33.5	
G. I write for other reasons besides school.	24.1	52.1	6.3	13.3	3.8
		76.3		17.2	
H. When I hand in a composition, I know I'm going to do poorly.	3.3	9.0	24.4	43.9	18.7
		12.3		62.6	
I. I enjoy writing.	19.7	39.1	18.2	14.8	7.6
		58.9		22.4	
J. I am afraid of writing essays when I know they will be evaluated.	6.8	22.0	25.9	33.9	10.9
		28.8		44.8	
K. I feel confident in my ability to clearly express my ideas in writing.	14.5	38.2	25.1	16.6	5.3
		52.7		21.9	
L. I avoid writing.	5.1	9.6	8.9	42.7	33.4
		14.8		76.1	

Percentages may not add to 100% due to nonresponse. Also, percentages for strongly agree and agree or disagree and strongly disagree may not add to total agreement or disagreement due to rounding.

Percentage of Respondents Giving a Positive Response to 12 Attitude Questions

At least 1	97.9%	At least 7	56.8%
At least 2	94.5	At least 8	43.8
At least 3	89.5	At least 9	32.9
At least 4	83.5	At least 10	22.3
At least 5	75.9	At least 11	11.8
At least 6	67.2	All 12	4.8

3 Feature: Teaching Practices

Theory: From Personality to Behavior to Subjects

Teaching theory is in such a sad state that those who do not teach K–12 and who have never (or rarely) taught K–12 are allowed to assert that their intuitive claims about K–12 teaching are superior to the insights of those who do teach. I call the claims of those who do not teach K–12 "intuitive" because such researchers, by and large, use a narrow, restricted sample of classroom data to make claims about the whole K–12 classroom, a set of data which they have not collected and in most cases not even observed. Thus, even though the data these researchers collect are governed by research norms, the data they speculate about are based on little more than intuition.

The data these researchers collect have been an inadequate representation of K–12 classrooms because these researchers have almost always focused on some single variable to the exclusion of everything else, whether teacher personality or teacher behavior, student behavior or subject content. Teacher personality studies ended with Nate Gage's conclusion that "these studies have yielded disappointing results" (1963, 118). The next focus was on either teacher or student behavior—for example, frequency of teacher-student interaction (Flanders 1967) and the academic learning time or time-on-task of students (Berliner 1976). Finally, some researchers turned to content and subject matter—for example, sequences of instruction in mastery learning (Bloom 1976) or the way teachers organized their subject matter (Schulman 1984).

By focusing their attention on a limited number of variables, these researchers have had much to say of interest. The problem starts when these studies are presumed to legitimize mandates to teachers about how to teach in all classrooms. Research on teaching has generally ignored anything that could not be measured by an observation instrument. In fact, the major book reviewing research on teaching explicitly rejects studies that do not have instruments for quantifying data (Dunkin and Biddle 1974, 3). As a result, studies of teaching have largely ignored the rich complexity of successful classrooms. For this reason and others, there are no adequate theories about teaching. In fact, one might say that studies of teaching have been generally atheoretical. One of the primary concerns of teachers is an adequate description of what brings about change in the classroom. The examples that follow are efforts in that direction.

Coding Practices and Patterns of Use

Some surveys of teaching practice use student evaluations. Below are samples of the student evaluation form and the overall results from Miriam Ylvisaker's class at Oakland High School:

Evaluate your writing now as compared with the beginning of this class:	Less	Same	Better
Ability to organize ideas			✔
Ability to express feelings in writing			✔
Ability to get ideas for what you want to say !		✔	
Your knowledge of vocabulary		✔	
Your knowledge of sentence structure			✔
Your knowledge of spelling			✔
Your over-all self-confidence about writing			✔✔✔

QUESTIONNAIRE *Evaluate your writing now as compared with the beginning of this course:*	Less	Same	Better
Ability to organize ideas		7	17
Ability to express feelings in writing		6	16
Ability to get ideas for what you want to say		8	14
Your knowledge of vocabulary		12	9
Your knowledge of sentence structure		11	10
Your knowledge of spelling		10	11
Your over-all self-confidence about writing	1	8	14
Evaluate this class	Not at all	Some-what	Very
Do you think making copies of students' writing is useful?	3	12	10
Do you think having students read aloud their writing is useful?	1	5	18
How much did you enjoy this class?	1	11	10
How useful do you consider this class?		5	15

Another sample of a survey of teaching practices is the questionnaire shown in table 13, given to seventeen-year-olds by NAEP (December 1980, 48–49).

Table 13

**Responses to Background Questions,
Age 17, 1974, 1979†**

	1974 (n = 34,211)	1979 (n = 26,651)	Change 1974–79
1. How many reports written in last 6 weeks as part of any school assignment?			
0	13.0%	13.9%	0.9%
1	11.4	12.3	1.0
2	16.3	16.8	0.4
3	14.7	14.0	−0.6
4	11.2	11.1	−0.1
5–10	25.7	22.5	−3.2
More than 10	6.2	5.3	−0.9
2. Time spent in English class on instruction in writing?			
None of the time	5.0	3.7	−1.3*
Little of the time	41.6	33.7*	−8.0*
1/3 of the time	33.6	31.7*	3.5*
1/2 of the time	13.8	17.4*	3.6*
Most of the time	5.8	6.9	1.1
3. A. Taken additional remedial writing course?			
Yes	6.3	8.2	1.9*
B. Taken additional creative writing course?			
Yes	20.5	24.6	4.1*
C. Taken other additional writing course?			
Yes	14.9	16.6	1.6
Total have taken at least one additional course other than remedial	26.1	24.0	−2.1
4. Encouraged to jot down ideas and take notes before writing?			
Usually		54.4	
Sometimes		35.1	
Never		7.7	

5. Encouraged to create outlines?

Usually	49.4	
Sometimes	35.5	
Never	11.2	

Encouraged to prewrite: notes or outlines or both 66.0

Neither notes nor outlines	31.2	
Either notes or outlines	28.3	
Both notes and outlines	37.7	

6. Do you draft papers more than once before turning in?

Usually	53.9	56.3	2.4
Sometimes	40.1	35.9	$-4.2*$
Never	5.9	7.8	$1.8*$

7. Does teacher write suggestions on paper?

Usually	33.1	48.0	$14.9*$
Sometimes	56.5	44.2	$-12.2*$
Never	10.4	7.7	$-2.7*$

8. Does teacher discuss papers with you?

Usually	27.0	
Sometimes	57.1	
Never	15.8	

Teacher feedback: written suggestions or discussion or both 57.9

Neither written suggestions nor discussion	42.1	
Either written suggestions or discussion	40.4	
Both written suggestions and discussion	17.5	

9. Do you work to improve papers after they are returned?

Usually	13.4	
Sometimes	46.2	
Never	40.3	

10. Do you enjoy working on writing assignments?

Usually	20.6	
Sometimes	55.3	
Never	24.1	

Summary of writing as a process:
Prewrite, draft, feedback, improve

None	10.4

At least one	89.5
At least two	67.0
At least three	34.2
All four	6.7

*Statistically significant at the .05 level.
†Percentages may not total due to rounding error.

Suggested Studies

1. What are student attitudes toward writing? Alberta Grossman, a teacher-researcher from the Virginia Writing Project, approached this question by keeping a journal on one student in class. Her journal includes the following entry (1982, 118):

> Mickey rereads what he has written, biting his pen tip, thinking. Then looks at his notes and writes again. I am writing too, trying to keep myself from being involved unless I am asked. Mickey has "gotten into" his "I-Search" on the Green Beret. He has skimmed old *Time* magazines, studied army recruitment materials, read Robin Moore's novel, *Green Beret*, and conducted two interviews. But I wonder if he's going to throw up his hands and say "forget the whole thing" now that he has to synthesize his information in writing. That's the way I feel whenever I get to that point in a research project.

> Mickey just looked up from his work . . . smiling! and beckoned to me. He was using the brief outline I gave him yesterday. He wanted to know what I mean by "give an honest assessment of the academic and personal qualifications you bring to Green Beret." I explained. He nodded. "Oh, O.K." and then WENT BACK TO WORK. HE HAS ALREADY BEEN WRITING FOR TWENTY MINUTES.

2. What are the writing practices at home and in school? Dan Hallford (1980), a teacher-researcher in the Bay Area Writing Project credential program, approached the first part of this question by surveying students on what writing and how much occurred at home. Terry Lillya (1979), Alyce Miller (1980), and Lawrence Sheppard (1982), also teacher-researchers in the Bay Area Writing Project's credential program, approached the second question by asking students to complete journals and surveys on the writing assigned and written in classes other than English.

Conclusion

I regard this book as part of the professionalization project now underway in this country for K–12 teachers. The goal of that project is a particular vision of what K–12 classroom teaching could be. In that vision, K–12 classroom teachers are regarded as the experts on K–12 classroom teaching, are assumed to be serious thinkers about teaching, and are assigned paid time outside the classroom to think about their teaching and the students in their classrooms.

In schools, the first opportunity for funded action research by K–12 teachers is typically the school assessment of writing under minimum competency statutes. A second opportunity is now available through the Research Foundation of the National Council of Teachers of English, which is accepting applications from classroom teachers for funds to do classroom research studies. Applicants should remember that these funds are not intended for research undertaken for a graduate degree program or for travel or purchase of permanent equipment. Recent proposals from teacher-researchers have focused on:

Effective strategies for peer evaluation (a comparison of different sets of responses from peers)

Strategies for learning to use word processors (a descriptive study of four elementary students' learning to use the word processor)

Themes in children's writing (a descriptive study of themes in the writing of six children, three boys and three girls, from kindergarten through third grade)

Teachers of grades K–12 are not going to get time off to think about their teaching unless they establish in some way the importance of such reflection, and teacher research is a way of beginning to establish such a tradition of inquiry among K–12 classroom teachers. It can provide examples illustrating the importance of teacher research. Examples of some of the kinds of positive impact teacher research can have on teaching are listed in appendix A, in a selection from an article by Marion Mohr, one of the country's major contributors to the K–12 teacher research movement. (I emphasize K–12 because college and university teachers have already established a tradition of inquiry.)

Finally, teacher research is one way of beginning to construct a vision of K–12 teaching in which school district assessments include case studies, and some faculty meetings and English department meetings include time for teachers to give progress reports on their research and to demonstrate lessons that work. Telling teachers they should do teacher research is, for me, an inadequate way to begin. A much more promising approach, in my experience, is to build teacher research projects into the school assessments which districts are willing to fund. The selling point for school districts is that after the papers have been holistically scored, the district needs to know some of the details about how students write in order to discuss intelligently the present writing program and its possible effects on students.

It is important that teacher research be shielded from some of the criticisms that researchers in the natural sciences level against one another. Teacher research needs a different set of norms, appropriate to the interests and working conditions of K–12 classroom teachers, and therefore I have insisted on a different name (teacher research) and a difference science (science of design). This insistence may strike some readers as odd, but I believe that the assumptions behind such distinctions will enable us to judge what a first-rate teacher-preparation program should be (and not be), and which research projects belong in the natural sciences and which properly belong in the area of inquiry among K–12 teachers.

Teachers who do teacher research will soon discover how difficult the whole business can be. One common reaction, after the first happiness over a trend (increasing T-units from low to high categories), is dissatisfaction with T-units, levels of generality, or stages—with language theory in general. George Miller's comments (1977, 181–82) on this point are helpful and at the same time an encouraging way to end this book:

> I do find depressing the short supply of theories adequate to support more insightful experimentation, but this depression is not mine alone. I have heard it expressed by several colleagues whose opinions I value. It is simply a fact: human languages are so complicated that good theories are hard to formulate. Without good theories, of course, only luck can guide us to make significant observations in the field or the laboratory. . . . Nobody ever promised us that science would be easy . . . I hope my emphasis on the difficulties will not obscure the real joy and pride we all felt in what was accomplished.

Appendix A
What Happened in Their Teaching?

Marian Mohr

1. Writing honestly about classroom problems, failures as well as successes, in a supportive atmosphere led to more self assurance and encouragement to change. The research logs, written under stress as they often were, in minutes between classes or during the times when the students themselves were writing, were honest writings, harsh sometimes, despairing sometimes. These writings and their authors were accepted by the other teachers and many found they shared the same problems. Teachers who avoided difficult questions about their teaching, who tried to avoid sharing their writings, were pulled up short by the other teachers in their response group. They would say to each other, "Maybe something else is going on. Have you thought about . . . ?" Being honest with themselves and with each other seemed to enable them to change. It was a difficult triple whammy—observing, writing, and analyzing what happened in their classes—a strain, as it was repeatedly described. It was also liberating.

2. Their research plans became their lesson plans. At first most felt they were working double, both teaching and conducting research. As the weeks passed, partly out of necessity to save time, but also out of response to their student responses, some changed their plans to make them more in line with what they were discovering. They began to see teaching more as a learning process rather than a daily routine or performance. One of the researchers[,] who was looking at writing to learn math, began to develop and change her math curriculum as she discovered more and more things that her students could do. A questionnaire would lead to another followed by an open class discussion that was taped and analyzed. Because they were more in touch with what their students were thinking, they did not plan in the same way that they had done previously. Tight[,] rigid lesson plans began to give. One

teacher invented a final exam that reflected her changed teaching ideas, met the requirements of her principal, and became part of her data. Another wove his data and findings back into his curriculum in a series of studies of American literature, at the same time recording the changes he himself was going through. For many their teaching and research became unified. One teacher wrote that she now "takes the lead from her students."

3. They switched from evaluating to documenting. Initially some expressed disappointment with their data, as if it were a lesson plan gone awry rather than simply what they were going to analyze. The switch to documenting was freeing and reassured teachers who were accustomed to being disappointed in the work of their students. Irritating classroom behavior, seen as data, became interesting. Error became a sign of growth.

4. They become more tolerant of creative chaos in their thinking (not in classroom behavior) and therefore more understanding of its appearance in their students' thinking and writing. One teacher called herself "a wishy washy Pisces researcher" as she continually refined and developed her research question. They knew from experience what it means to discover your idea gradually as you write and do research. Revision became a commonplace, a fact of life. One teacher reported a sense of "messiness" as part of her teaching, another that she felt she was "fluttering around hither and thither" as she did her research. Although the teachers were not completely comfortable with these feelings, they were acknowledged as part of the process and therefore as legitimate parts of the process of learning of their students.

5. They changed the focus from teaching students to finding out what their students knew and then trying to help them learn. One teacher wrote "I'm to the point where I ask them before I ask them." They discovered that their students knew more and could learn more than they had imagined. They reported asking more questions, listening more, and respecting the worries and concerns of the students as legitimate, waiting, rather than rushing in with a suggestion. They received the cooperation and interest of their students in their research. In some cases the students became partners in the project. The students became more aware of their own learning and writing processes. One student chose her own research name. Many of them read the drafts of the reports and made comments to the teacher-researcher. The teachers and

their students became learners together and the students began to see their teachers as learners. The teacher-researcher modeled the learning process for his or her students.

6. The teachers were able to try new ways of teaching because they were very sensitive to the classroom variables. While researching, they were examining the context simultaneously with the teaching. Perhaps what happens with some attempts at teacher change is that even though teachers accept new ideas presented in an interesting, authentic and enthusiastic manner, if the ideas are not compatible with their classroom context, they will not work as they did at the inservice program. During research, however, the context is an examined integral part of the practice and the teacher is receiving constant response from students concerning the context, so that the idea gets a full trial.

7. As a teacher of teacher-researchers, I found the same changes taking place in myself I noticed happening to them. We became colleagues learning together. I made honest and direct comments and responses to them about their work. I took more notes on what they said and talked less. On January 20 I noted in my log,"I'm developing a new teaching technique—sending out comments when they're too late to do any good and having them reaffirm what the researchers have already figured out for themselves." This happened accidentally at first because of the many times I returned comments to the teachers later than I had planned. I know that I was helpful to them on some occasions, and they helped me with the material I'm putting together for this article. I'm not sure how permanent the changes are, but I know that I felt uncomfortable with some of the teaching I was doing in another course for teachers and I began to modify what I was doing there as well.

One teacher who helped me by giving comments on this article in process asked, "Are you going to say how hard it was?" It was hard because of the circumstances under which we were working and because we were new at it. One January night after I got home from class I received a phone call from one of the teachers who said, "It's the first night I haven't been tired since the vacation." We worked hard, but it was a different kind of tired.

(From Marian M. Mohr, *Window Sill: Teacher-Researchers and the Study of Writing Process*)

Appendix B
Evaluation Designs for Practitioners

Maurice J. Eash

Harriet Talmage

Herbert J. Walberg

Planning and implementing any facet of the educational program call for decision making whether the project concerns the program of an entire school system or the day-to-day practice of a teacher in a single classroom. The interactive nature of the educational process produces a dynamic environment; hence, decisions made at one point in time require reassessment at the next point in time before another round of decisions can begin. Evaluation provides a framework for building a systematic data base to aid in making decisions in school and classroom practice. With an appropriate data base, problems can be reformulated, both potential and actual consequences can be analyzed, and, as a result, the processes can be redirected.

Practitioners are not afforded the luxury of ideal laboratory conditions. The natural settings of the classroom, the school, or the school system place constraints upon the type of data obtainable; hence, educators must work with less than an ideal experimental design.[1]

Four evaluation designs used in natural settings are described in the following sections.[2] Each involves an evaluation study that takes into account a variety of constraints, but nevertheless provides a basis for subsequent program and/or organizational decisions. The studies range from a true experimental design, one that necessitates the random assignment of students to experimental and control groups, to a design that lacks both randomization and comparative groups.

In each section, the basic paradigm of the evaluation design is symbolically presented. Four symbols identify the elements of the paradigms: R—randomization; X—treatment; O—observation; and in some cases, DA—design analysis. Subscripts denote specific treatments and observations. Observations (O) to the left of the treatment (X) denote pretest data, and to the right, posttest data. The experimental group symbols appear above the control group symbols. A broken line between the groups indicates nonequivalent groups.

A True Experimental Design in a Field Setting	R × O
	R O

A true experimental design is characterized by its randomization of subjects to treatment—"randomly dividing the litter among treatments"— and is the conventional laboratory-science way of exercising this control. The strength of the design, randomization for control of error, is also a major source of difficulty in field evaluations because studies are conducted where scheduling, teacher preferences in assignment, luncheon arrangements, and a myriad of other considerations enter in. Thus one finds the experimental design infrequently used in reported evaluations. However, because of its power to bring forth more valid findings, we suggest that evaluators search for ways to employ it in field situations. An example drawn from an evaluation of a curriculum model set up under a Title III grant illustrates the power of a true experimental design to bare true differences and the weaknesses of nonrandom comparison groups. Clocktown, a fast growing suburb in a major metropolitan area, received a three-year grant to design a middle school curriculum which would break sharply with the conventional curriculum in the seven other junior high schools. The new curriculum included: 1) greater parent involvement, 2) a more humanistic orientation, 3) promoting greater achievement, 4) promoting more affective growth, 5) integrating pupil personnel services within the curriculum, and 6) offering these changes at a per-pupil cost competitive with the costs in the other junior high schools. After one year of planning, the two-year experimental school opened.

Through a combination of events and advanced planning, a true experimental design became possible. A pool of 600 potential students for the Model School was developed through volunteers and recruitment. The Model School was established to enroll 300 students, and all applicants were informed that a random selection would govern admission to the school. The outside evaluators randomly selected the 300 students, thereby creating an experimental group (those in the Model School) and control groups (those who were in the original pool of applicants but were not admitted to the school).

A number of measurements were taken to evaluate the goals of the Model School. Whenever possible, the results were analyzed within the experimental designs of Experimental Group vs. Control Group. One example of the strength of the experimental design over a quasi-experimental comparison group design is shown in Figure 1, where achievement test scores for the Model School, the Control Schools students, and the district average for all junior high school eighth graders are graphed. This graph shows dramatic differences in curriculum treatment between the experimental and the control groups in selected areas of mathematics and reading achievement. If the district averages had been substituted for the control group results, much of the effect of the curriculum change would have been obscured, for clearly the achievement of the pool of students is not representative of the district's average achievement.

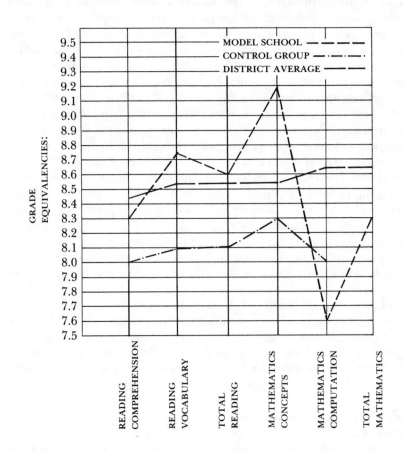

Figure 1. Reading and Mathematics SRA Achievement Grade Equivalencies for Grade 8: Model School, Control Group, and District Average

A second example of how true differences are masked is seen when a volunteer group instead of a randomly selected control group is used in a comparison of classroom observations made in volunteer teachers' classrooms. In year two, the control group of classrooms to be observed was randomly selected to obtain a more representative sample of classroom practice to compare with the Model School. The differences are much sharper since the first year volunteer control group classrooms were much closer to the experimental group in practice than were the typical district junior high school classrooms. (See Figure 2.) The ex-

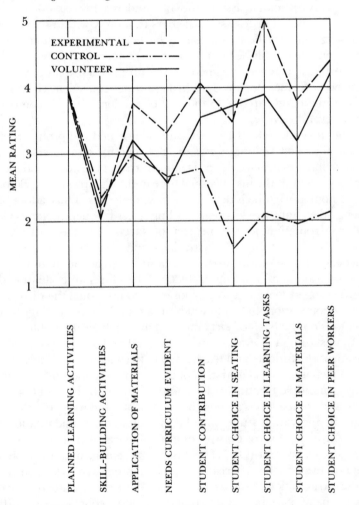

Figure 2. Mean Ratings for Randomly Selected Experimental Classrooms, Control Classrooms, and Volunteer Classrooms

perimental design is invaluable to control error and to trace the attri-
bution of results to treatment more clearly. Every effort should be made
to use it when the question of curriculum effects is at issue or a summative evaluation is at stake.

Nonequivalent Control-Group Design

$O \times O$
$O \times O$

It is usually difficult to assign students randomly to classrooms receiving
special treatment or to assign teachers randomly within schools to special programs. In the first instance, parents tend to resist changes that
vary from the established curriculum without their approval. In the second instance, teachers assigned to new programs involuntarily may affect the outcomes negatively. Through a nonequivalent control-group
design, the handicap due to the lack of randomization is compensated
for in several ways.

The Textville School District study concerned the problems of evaluating four new reading series to select one for system-wide adoption.
Instructional materials play a significant role in the educational process
for 75 percent of the instructional time in the classroom, and 90 percent
of the homework time is devoted to these materials. Thus, adoption cannot be taken lightly. Selecting a reading series frequently entails ideological confrontation to the neglect of facts. Publishers display their
materials with attractive illustrations and slick copy, and groups of
teachers espouse one approach to reading instruction or another as the
final solution to all reading problems. Therefore, an evaluation design
was developed to serve two purposes: 1) to overcome the difficulties of
nonrandomization and 2) to establish a data base for making selection
decisions on the basis of facts rather than ideological quibbling.

In designing the evaluation study, the drawbacks of nonrandom assignment of students and teachers to experimental and control groups
were taken into consideration by obtaining pretest and posttest data, em-
ploying multiple treatments for comparisons with the traditional treatment and comparisons among the treatments, and using the class rather
than the individual student as the unit of study. An adaptation of the
nonequivalent control-group design is illustrated in Figure 3. Pretest
(O_{preT}) and posttest (O_{postT}) reading achievement data were obtained.
Data on teacher characteristics (O_1) were initially collected. Subsequent
to the introduction of the treatment (X), data were obtained on learning
environment variables (O_2: competitiveness, cohesiveness, difficulty,
friction, and satisfaction) and on instructional characteristics (O_3: locus

O_{preT}	O_1	X_1	O_{postT}	O_2	O_3
O_{preT}	O_1	X_2	O_{postT}	O_2	O_3
O_{preT}	O_1	X_3	O_{postT}	O_2	O_3
O_{preT}	O_1	X_4	O_{postT}	O_2	O_3
O_{preT}	O_1	$X_{control}$	O_{postT}	O_2	O_3

Figure 3. Nonequivalent Control-Group Design Paradigm

of instructional decisions, variety and utilization of materials, and student behaviors).

The Textville schools and teachers were encouraged to participate in the study. Sixty classes from 12 schools were chosen and represented the range of ability, of socioeconomic, racial, and ethnic backgrounds, and of geographic locations found in the district. Assignment to a reading series by grade level is shown in Figure 4. For each reading series, the materials were field-tested in three different schools in grades 1, 2, 3, and 6. In all, the data included 12 different classes per series.

Two constraints were imposed on the design: 1) All four classes in a school field-testing the reading materials must use the same series; and 2) the best educational interest of the students must supersede the design of the study. And, indeed, this came to pass: One class found too many difficulties with the series at the peril of impeding their reading progress, and the class was removed from the study.

The data were analyzed to provide information on four questions:

- Do the classes using one series obtain higher reading scores on the reading achievement posttest than classes using another series?

- Do the classes using one reading series perceive their learning environment differently than do classes using another reading series? Do the learning environment and reading series taken together affect achievement?

GRADE LEVEL	SERIES X_1	SERIES X_2	SERIES X_3	SERIES X_4	SERIES $X_{control}$	TOTAL
1st	3	3	3	3	3	15
2nd	3	3	3	3	3	15
3rd	3	3	3	3	3	15
6th	3	3	3	3	3	15
TOTAL CLASSES	12	12	12	12	12	60

Figure 4. Assignment to Treatment Matrix

- Do selected teacher characteristics in conjunction with a given series affect reading achievement?

- Does instruction differ in classes using different reading series?

Statistical analyses indicated that the pretest score is the single most significant predictor of reading achievement despite teacher characteristics and regardless of the reading series. After the effects of the pretest scores are removed, competitiveness is the only other variable that predicts reading achievement. The higher the competitiveness in the learning environment, the lower the reading achievement. There are no significant correlations between competitiveness and reading series, teacher characteristics, or instructional characteristics.

The final selection decision for the Textville School District shifted away from an emphasis on ideological issues such as phonics-oriented vs. nonphonics-oriented reading approaches or linguistic vs. nonlinguistic reading approaches. In place of these, attention was focused on the instructional aspects of a reading program that tend to reduce competitiveness, and on such concerns as the district's philosophy of reading, cost factors, implementation problems, and the degree of teacher dependence on outside support.

	1972 1973		1973 1974	
Time-Series Design	O X	O	O X	O

Practitioners are frequently faced with the necessity of making major program changes which reorganize curriculum and structural arrangements. Not infrequently, such changes are precipitated by external forces that are impatient with the setting up of an evaluation design that would require the establishing of control groups before the change is made. In these cases, data are frequently desperately needed by administrative decision makers if they are not to be at the mercy of rumor and pressure groups. Such was the case of the Parkland School District, which was suddenly under a legal mandate to integrate its schools. *De facto* segregation resulting from segregated housing placed practically all the black population in one elementary school and the white population in six schools, and produced segregation up through grade 6. The junior high schools were integrated in name, but not always in reality, for the students segregated themselves by race in the lunchroom and on the playground. Faced with a legal mandate to bus students to achieve equal racial proportions in all seven elementary schools, Parkland administrators requested an outside evaluator to help them set up an evaluation design that would provide basic data on these questions: 1) What effects does the structural reorganization required by busing have on student achievement and on the learning environment? 2) What data would be useful for program planning and for alerting the administration to potential difficulties?

The evaluation was hampered by the inability to set up control groups through randomization. Moreover, since the entire school system was involved, no separate control groups were available. Within these limitations, it was decided to use a time-series design for a two-year period that would allow within-the-group comparisons, use a multiple collection of data, and give a reading on several indices of progress. Experience indicates that over the two years many productive hypotheses were generated and an invaluable data base for charting progress in achievement, race relations, and classroom instruction was established.

A pretest and posttest on general achievement was given every child in the fall and spring. Since there were previous local norms available, these data quieted fears that integration was destroying achievement. A learning environment measure, administered in the spring, revealed that further curriculum planning was needed to improve the learning environment for both white and black students in different schools. An analysis of the learning environment and achievement measures revealed that some schools appeared to be much more successful than others in providing a stimulating learning environment and promoting achievement. While the lack of adequate controls limited generalizations or conclusions, these data did pinpoint areas for closer investigation by administrators and teachers. One of the more immediately useful applications of evaluation data came when rumors of the deterioration of discipline in one school swept the community. The recently administered learning environment inventory profile calmed both the school board and the public by its demonstration that the students in this school perceived their environment very much as did their counterparts in other schools, and that there was no greater conflict or disruption in their school than in the others.

A third area of data was an analysis of the records of disciplinary cases in the junior high schools. These again provided some short-term data as the basis of decisions, since the offenses that took up most of administrators' and guidance counselors' time were being committed by a very small group of students. (See Figure 5.) Interracial problems were not as prevalent as intraracial problems. A second year of charting these

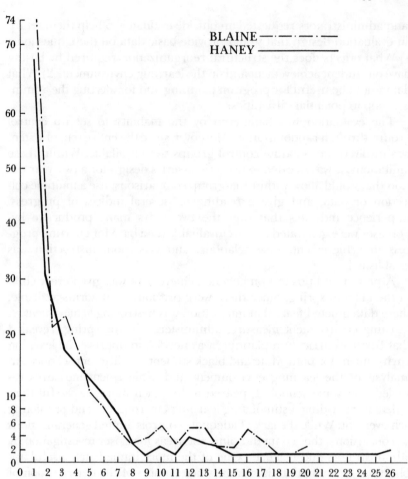

Figure 5. Summary Graph of Frequencies of Behavioral Incidents

behavioral incidents showed that the concentration of social services on
the few major offenders had removed them from the behavioral records
in the second year. In addition, it was found that interracial conflict had
decreased. Thus, one is led to conclude that the time-series design provides a useful data base for decision making in a situation where tensions
induced by structural changes cry for the voice of rationality. One must
admit that these data have limited generalizability, but they have been
invaluable in the context in which they are collected and in demonstrat-
ing that evaluation can serve several purposes in applied settings.

No Comparison Group Design	Design Analysis	X — O X — O Design Analysis X — O

Not infrequently, an evaluator is confronted with a program that is to be used but is being undertaken with restraints that forestall the use of control groups. Is usefulness of evaluation forestalled under these circumstances, and must one retreat to the rhetoric of castigating shortsightedness in the developer? The fourth example deals with such a problem.

An outside private agency provided funds to increase and improve the teaching of the arts in schools. Launched from very broad objectives, "to enable parents and community leaders to use the arts as communication tools," the agency requested evaluation assistance to improve the series of workshops that it had designed for teachers.

From the workshops' guides that were presented and from the funding proposal, an analysis of workshop activities to achieve the goals was prepared. The activities proved to be a better source of goals than the diffuse general objectives. The evaluation design was concerned with: 1) Were the activities being taught in the workshops? 2) Were they perceived as useful by teachers since they incorporated creative and nonconventional teaching approaches? 3) Were they being implemented in classrooms and did they maintain the integrity of the activities?

The evaluators were not permitted to gather data from control classes in the schools, nor were they to observe the instructors assigned to the workshops. The design of the evaluation structured the gathering of data by analyzing the program and developing an activity analysis, which was then converted into an instrument to be used by teachers to evaluate workshop activities on four dimensions: 1) the workshop participants' reaction, 2) whether teachers used any one activity in the classroom, 3) the students' reactions, and 4) ease of implementation. A second source of data was gathered from a pretest and a posttest of learning environments in the workshop participants' classrooms. A third source of data was observation in classrooms where teachers taught the workshop activities to their students. A fourth source of data was a standardized teacher evaluation questionnaire to evaluate the workshops.

From these data an analysis was made of the workshops, and recommendations were rendered on which workshops and what activities were most useful in the classroom. As this evaluation progressed, feedback sessions were held with workshop directors to assist them in conducting the next semester's workshops. Evaluation in this case focused on providing clarity to a group of program developers who were working in an ambiguous area. Although many of the traditional parameters of an evaluation design are lacking, these are data that can be generated and comparisons that can be made to shape the educational product. In the sense of serving to improve practice through the establishment of a data base and promoting meaningful comparisons for practitioners, the evaluation design remains true to its calling in bringing rationality to play on educational activities.

Cooperative Planning in Evaluation

Evaluation is often viewed by practitioners as being outside their reach: The designs are incomprehensible, the data are too costly to gather, the participants are threatened by the potential of the findings, and the effects, efforts, and efficiency cannot be evaluated with any degree of objectivity anyway. Our experience, gathered over a wide variety of projects, would indicate that practitioners are handicapped by too narrow a view of evaluation and by their failure to systematically build an evaluation design into projects. Moreover, troublesome problems are not approached through an evaluation design which in its use converts rhetoric to a factual base, as was illustrated in the example on the reading series. In short, decision making and choice taking are blind through the lack of evaluation designs which open up options and permit an earlier use of correctives in program planning.

To provide for an evaluation design in the early stages makes for a more open commitment to the major goals of a project, and establishes a degree of latitude for shifting direction based on evidence which often is denied when the program participants' personal commitments to a project deepen with effort. Evaluation can serve to keep the focus on the quest for a better way to provide education as opposed to espousing a dogma of "the way to provide quality education." If evaluation is seen as a necessary part of projects and problem solving, the use of evaluators and evaluation findings becomes as significant as the appropriate use of evaluation designs. Findings must be implemented to be effective in decision making.

At the Office of Evaluation Research, we have found that cementing an early working relationship between the evaluators and the practitioners is the best guarantee of the use of evaluation findings. As outside evaluators, this entails building an evaluation design early in the project with inputs from practitioners on their needs for data. In another context, we have referred to this process as a *coactional relationship*[3] where the two parties are engaged in a mutual task with a commitment to the discovery of options and the search for truth. Extra effort is required from the evaluators to explain designs and their strengths and constraints; but these early sessions also build the foundation of commitment to follow the findings wherever they may lead. The process is coactional in that the evaluators perceive the context in which the evaluation design is being used and it is early on plans for implementation of findings at appropriate junctures. Our contention is that many evaluation reports are superfluous because they are ill-timed to the schedule of information needs of practitioners, or return findings that are arcane and remote from the decisions that are pressing the decision maker. We see, as imperative to success, the need to be sensitive to the roles of the evaluators and practitioners and their relationships in building evaluation designs. The four evaluation designs described illustrate applications of a methodology in a field context. Brevity did not permit the description of roles and relationships, though they are implicit in the applications. Appropriate use of evaluation designs, we contend, can bring rationality into play in field-based problems and can improve educational practice.

TM Report 35, published in December, 1974, by the ERIC Clearinghouse on Tests, Measurement, and Evaluation, Princeton, New Jersey 08540.

Notes

1. The studies used to illustrate the designs were conducted by the Office of Evaluation Research, College of Education, University of Illinois at Chicago Circle.
2. For additional designs, the reader may wish to consult Donald T. Campbell and Julian C. Stanley, *Experimental and Quasi-Experimental Designs for Research.* Chicago: Rand McNally Company, 1963.
3. Maurice J. Eash, "Transactional Evaluation of Classroom Practice," in *Studies in Transactional Evaluation,* ed. Robert M. Rippey. Berkeley: McCuchan Pub. Corp., 1973.

Appendix C
A Note on Sampling
and Statistical Tests

Random sampling can help the action researcher keep a project within the resources available in schools. If the assumption is that the features counted in a sample represent what one would expect to find in the given population, then the sample must be drawn randomly from the given population. In simple random sampling, each paper in the population has a unique two-digit number, and individual sample papers are selected by choosing two-digit numbers from the table of random numbers below. Where one begins on the table is arbitrary. If one begins in the upper right corner and goes down, the first four numbers are 51, 26, 68, and 12. If a number does not appear in the population, ignore it. The size of the sample should be based on some estimate of the diversity within the population. For a class of 30 with a great range of skills, select 28 papers. For a school district population of 8,000 with a great range of skills, select 367 papers if possible. These estimates come from a best-case formula in Krejcie and Morgan (1970). But best-case is not always possible. In any circumstance, try to get at least 5 samples for each skill you want to discuss. The point of sample size is that if all the students in a population are exactly alike, a sample of one is just fine. That one will produce results representative of the population in question. Because students are not exactly alike, however, the general rule of sample size is that more is usually better. But more requires more time.

Random Numbers

1368	9621	9151	2066	1208	2664	9822	6599	6911	5112
5953	5936	2541	4011	0408	3593	3679	1378	5936	2651
7226	9466	9553	7671	8599	2119	5337	5953	6355	6889
8883	3454	6773	8207	5576	6386	7487	0190	0867	1298
7022	5281	1168	4099	8069	8721	8353	9952	8006	9045
4576	1853	7884	2451	3488	1286	4842	7719	5795	3953
8715	1416	7028	4616	3470	9938	5703	0196	3465	0034
4011	0408	2224	7626	0643	1149	8834	6429	8691	0143
1400	3694	4482	3608	1238	8221	5129	6105	5314	8385
6370	1884	0820	4854	9161	6509	7123	4070	6759	6113

4522	5749	8084	3932	7678	3549	0051	6761	6952	7041
7195	6234	6426	7148	9945	0358	3242	0519	6550	1327
0054	0810	2937	2040	2299	4198	0846	3937	3986	1019
5166	5433	0381	9686	5670	5129	2103	1125	3404	8785
1247	3793	7415	7819	1783	0506	4878	7673	9840	6629
8529	7842	7203	1844	8619	7404	4215	9969	6948	5643
8973	3440	4366	9242	2151	0244	0922	5887	4883	1177
9307	2959	5904	9012	4951	3695	4529	7197	7179	3239
2923	4276	9467	9868	2257	1925	3382	7244	1781	8037
6372	2808	1238	8098	5509	4617	4099	6705	2386	2830
6922	1807	4900	5306	0411	1828	8634	2331	7247	3230
9862	8336	6453	0545	6127	2741	5967	8447	3017	5709
3371	1530	5104	3076	5506	3101	4143	5845	2095	6127
6712	9402	9588	7019	9248	9192	4223	6555	7947	2474
3071	8782	7157	5941	8830	8563	2252	8109	5880	9912
4022	9734	7852	9096	0051	7387	7056	9331	1317	7833
9682	8892	3577	0326	5306	0050	8517	4376	0788	5443
6705	2175	9904	3743	1902	5393	3032	8432	0612	7972
1872	8292	2366	8603	4288	6809	4357	1072	6822	5611
2559	7534	2281	7351	2064	0611	9613	2000	0327	6145
4399	3751	9783	5399	5175	8894	0296	9483	0400	2272
6074	8827	2195	2532	7680	4288	6807	3101	6850	6410
5155	7186	4722	6721	0838	3632	5355	9369	2006	7681
3193	2800	6184	7891	9838	6123	9397	4019	8389	9508
8610	1880	7423	3384	4625	6653	2900	6290	9286	2396
4778	8818	2992	6300	4239	9595	4384	0611	7687	2088
3987	1619	4164	2542	4042	7799	9084	0278	8422	4330
2977	0248	2793	3351	4922	8878	5703	7421	2054	4391
1312	2919	8220	7285	5902	7882	1403	5354	9913	7109
3890	7193	7799	9190	3275	7840	1872	6232	5295	3148
0793	3468	8762	2492	5854	8430	8472	2264	9279	2128
2139	4552	3444	6462	2524	8601	3372	1848	1472	9667
8277	9153	2880	9053	6880	4284	5044	8931	0861	1517
2236	4778	6639	0862	9509	2141	0208	1450	1222	5281
8837	7686	1771	3374	2894	7314	6856	0440	3766	6047
6605	6380	4599	3333	0713	8401	7146	8940	2629	2006
8399	8175	3525	1646	4019	8390	4344	8975	4489	3423
8053	3046	9102	4515	2944	9763	3003	3408	1199	2791
9837	9378	3237	7016	7593	5958	0068	3114	0456	6840
2557	6395	9496	1884	0612	8102	4402	5498	0422	3335

It is also recommended, if possible, to use appropriate statistical tests to determine when pre/post or other comparison numbers are asserted to be significantly different. In this case, significant difference means that the difference between the two numbers is not a matter of chance and, therefore, may be attributable to other causes. If the comparison numbers are based on a continuous scale (1, 23, 55, 37, 9, 103), the t-test can be used to determine statistical significance.

A t-test has three parts: (1) two means or average scores from two groups or two tests of the same group (average number of words in groups A and B), posttest scores from groups A and B or repeated measures of the same group with pretest being A and the posttest being B); (2) the variance in groups or tests A and B, showing the range or dispersion of a group's scores around the mean or average; and (3) sample size. Many hand calculators will provide the mean and variance for each group if all of the individual scores in the sample are entered. The formula for the t-test is as follows:

$$t = \frac{\text{Difference between two means}}{\sqrt{\dfrac{\text{Variance of sample A}}{\text{Size of sample A}} + \dfrac{\text{Variance of sample B}}{\text{Size of sample B}}}}$$

$$= \frac{\text{Difference between two means}}{\text{Standard error of the difference}}$$

The difference between the two means is then divided by the standard error of the difference, a measure of the dispersion and range of scores in the two samples, and the result is the t-statistic. When the t-statistic has been calculated, the researcher must consult a t-table to find the value of the t-statistic. First, find the degrees of freedom (total students in the sample minus the number of groups) and find the column for a 5 percent chance of error. It is a convention among statisticians to accept as tolerable a 5 percent chance of error. Notice that a 1 percent chance of error is a harder standard to meet, requiring a higher t-value.

If the degrees of freedom are twenty-eight, then the t-value in the 5 percent error column is 2.048. This means that the t-statistic calculated using the formula above must be greater than 2.048 in order to be statistically significant.

The assumption of the t-test is that the two groups being compared are comparable and come from essentially the same population. If it turns out that from the very beginning one group was obviously more skillful than another, then an analysis of covariance can be used to adjust scores so that groups are comparable. Ask for help with this.

Values of *t* at the 5% and 1% Levels of Significance

Degrees of Freedom	5%	1%	Degrees of Freedom	5%	1%
1	12.706	63.657	32	2.037	2.739
2	4.303	9.925	34	2.032	2.728
3	3.182	5.841	36	2.027	2.718
4	2.776	4.604	38	2.025	2.711
5	2.571	4.032	40	2.021	2.704
6	2.447	3.707	42	2.017	2.696
7	2.365	3.499	44	2.015	2.691
8	2.306	3.355	46	2.012	2.685
9	2.262	3.250	48	2.010	2.681
10	2.228	3.169	50	2.008	2.678
11	2.201	3.106	55	2.005	2.668
12	2.179	3.055	60	2.000	2.660
13	2.160	3.012	65	1.998	2.653
14	2.145	2.977	70	1.994	2.648
15	2.131	2.947	80	1.990	2.638
16	2.120	2.921	90	1.987	2.632
17	2.110	2.898	100	1.984	2.626
18	2.101	2.878	125	1.979	2.616
19	2.093	2.861	150	1.976	2.609
20	2.086	2.845	200	1.972	2.601
21	2.080	2.831	300	1.968	2.592
22	2.074	2.819	400	1.966	2.588
23	2.069	2.807	500	1.965	2.586
24	2.064	2.797	1000	1.962	2.581
25	2.060	2.787	∞	1.960	2.576
26	2.056	2.779			
27	2.052	2.771			
28	2.048	2.763			
29	2.045	2.756			
30	2.042	2.750			

(Reprinted with permission of the Free Press, a division of Macmillan, Inc. from *Statistical Methods for Research Workers,* 14th ed., by Ronald A. Fisher. © 1970 University of Adelaide.)

T-tests are used for measurements along some continuous scale. However, some measurements are binomial, a two-sided yes/no, disagree/agree, or pass/fail measurement. In these cases, the numbers are the frequencies for each side. The most commonly used statistic for data in the form of frequencies is the chi-square (X^2). The basic idea of chi-square is that when two answers are available, the chances are that the frequencies will split 50/50. Thus, in a class of 30, 15 should answer "yes" and 15 should answer "no." If 20 answer "yes" and 10 answer "no," then chi-square will indicate whether or not the difference between the two answers is still within the realm of chance or outside the realm of chance and thus statistically significant. Many hand calculators provide the means to calculate chi-square values.

Numbers are used for different purposes—some to number a scale (nominal, ordinal, interval, and ratio), others to describe a tendency (mean, median, and mode), still others to show distribution, and others to show relationships. These are defined below. Two of the critical measures are the averages, showing a central tendency, and the measures of dispersion, showing the range among scores. The chart on pages 148–49 summarizes the use of these two types of measures.

Overview of Statistical Methods

A. Numbers and Their Use
    1. Nominal Scale—in place of a name (to identify).
    2. Ordinal Scale—to indicate order (to rank).
    3. Interval Scale—to indicate equal intervals (to add and subtract).
    4. Ratio Scale—to indicate ratio (to multiply and divide).
B. Central Tendency ("Averages")
    1. Mean
    2. Median
    3. Mode
C. Distribution (Spread)
    1. Standard Deviation and Variance
    2. Semi-interquartile Range $\left(\dfrac{Q_3 - Q_1}{2} \right)$
    3. Range
        $\left(\dfrac{\text{Range}}{6} \cong \text{(one standard deviation when } N \cong 100) \right)$
D. Comparisons and Relationships between Numbers
    1. *Simple Correlation*—measures the degree of relationship between two variables. May be positive (direct) or negative (indirect or inverse).
    2. *Partial Correlation*—involves the relationship between two variables in a situation where three or more variables are present, holding one or more variables constant and allowing the others to vary.
    3. *Multiple Correlation*—involves the correlation between a dependent variable (or a criterion variable) and an optimally weighted combination of two or more independent (predictor) variables.

4. *Factor Analysis*—a technique for analyzing patterns of intercorrelation among many variables, isolating the dimensions to account for these patterns of correlation and, in a well-designed study, to allow inferences concerning the psychological nature of the construct represented by the dimension.

5. $\bar{z}$-*Ratio* or *t-Ratio*—test the (null) hypothesis that two samples come from two populations with the same mean and differ only because of sampling error. ($\bar{z}$ applies to populations with or without equal variances; t assumes the population variances are equal.)

6. *Analysis of Variance*—tests one or more (null) hypotheses that the means of all groups sampled come from populations with equal means and differ only because of sampling error. (F test: the technique used in Analysis of Variance which compares the Between-group variance to the Within-group variance.)

7. *Chi-square*—a measure of squared deviations between observed and theoretical numbers in terms of frequencies in categories or cells of a table, determining whether such deviations are due to sampling error or some interdependence or correlation among the frequencies. It involves a comparison of frequencies of two or more corresponding groups. Very useful in tables involving frequencies of Yes-No answers.

(From William B. Michael and Stephen Isaac, *Handbook in Research and Evaluation*, 2d ed., copyright 1981 by EdITS Publishers, San Diego, California 92107. Reprinted by permission.)

Measures of Central Tendency and Variability

A. When to use the three averages:
1. Compute the arithmetic *mean* when:
   a. The greatest reliability is wanted. It usually varies less from sample to sample drawn from the same population.
   b. Other computations, as finding measures of variability, are to follow.
   c. The distribution is symmetrical about the center, and especially when it is approximately normal.
   d. We wish to know the "center of gravity" of a sample.
2. Compute the *median* when:
   a. There is not sufficient time to compute the mean.
   b. Distributions are markedly skewed. This includes the case in which one or more extreme measurements are at one side of the distribution.
   c. We are interested in whether cases fall within the upper or lower halves of the distribution and not particularly in how far from the central point.
   d. An incomplete distribution is given.

3. Compute the *mode* when:
    a. The quickest estimate of central value is wanted.
    b. A rough estimate of central value will do.
    c. We wish to know what is the most typical case.

B. When to use the three measures of dispersion:
    1. Use the *range* when:
        a. The quickest possible index of dispersion is wanted.

            $$\frac{\text{Range}}{6} \cong \text{one standard deviation when } N \geqslant 100$$

        b. Information is wanted concerning extreme scores.
    2. Use the *semi-interquartile range, Q,* (see preceding page) when:
        a. The median is the only statistic of central value reported.
        b. The distribution is truncated or incomplete at either end.
        c. There are a few very extreme scores or there is an extreme skewing.
        d. We want to know the actual score limits of the middle 50 percent of the cases.
    3. Use the *standard deviation* when:
        a. Greatest dependability of the value is wanted.
        b. Further computations that depend upon it are likely to be needed.
        c. Interpretations related to the normal distribution curve are desired.

        (Note: The standard deviation has a number of useful relationships to the normal curve and to other statistical concepts.)

(From J. P. Guilford, *Fundamental Statistics in Psychology and Education,* 4th ed. Copyright McGraw-Hill Book Company, New York, 1965. Reprinted by permission of McGraw-Hill Book Company.)

Appendix D
Using Expressive Writing
to Teach Biology

Robert Tierney

Introduction

Though most high school biology teachers agree, to some extent, that all teachers should be teachers of writing, they are often reluctant to include student writing exercises, beyond normal transactional reporting,[1] in their programs. Biology teachers point, with some pride, to the numerous lab write-ups, student reports, and tests they have corrected for grammar, spelling, and neatness as their contribution to the improvement of writing. Expressive writing, the language used in friendly talk, or the writing which takes place during the initial phase of thinking through a problem, is best left to the English teacher down the hall. After all, they reason, English teachers are trained for that sort of thing.

Probably the primary reason for not including expressive writing in the biology class is lack of time. Time devoted to the teaching of writing is time lost for biology; there isn't enough time to present all of the biological subject matter that should be presented. Biology teachers, like most teachers, find themselves forced to make value judgments about which topics to delete, and they sometimes feel guilty about their decisions afterward. How can one justify a skimming over of the Echinoderms, or short-changing the Kreb's Cycle?

Another reason for not emphasizing writing in the biology class is the paperwork load. As it is, most biology programs include labs every week, and labs mean lab reports or workbooks to be corrected. Add to the lab write-ups a few student reports, a notebook, and other assignments, and it means confronting a stack of uncorrected papers that would intimidate even the most dedicated tutor.

Probably the saddest reason for not including expressive writing is many biology teachers fail to realize its potential as a learning tool because they are not familiar with writing as a process. Few biology teachers are themselves writers. Yet modern biology instruction requires a hands-on, inquiry, think-through-the-problem approach. Expressive writing is a means of thinking through a problem. The student is free to do his [or her] thinking on paper without fear of the teacher as an examiner. Expressive writing can provide the biology student with the essential experience of free inquiry—the essence of the scientific method.

The biology student who is allowed time, and encouraged, to write expressively about what he [or she] has been presented in biology will be a better student. He [or she] will have a more thorough understanding of the biological concepts and will experience both the pain and the thrill of problem solving. Certainly his [or her] reports will be more interesting for the teacher to read, and that, in itself, might make the effort worthwhile.

This experiment is an attempt to suggest some techniques for including expressive writing in the biology class and to objectively evaluate their potential. Perhaps it will encourage other biology teachers to try some of the ideas, refine them, or develop new ones.

Background

The School

Irvington High School, built in 1961, is situated in the suburban community of Fremont on the southeastern shore of San Francisco Bay. It is one of four high schools in a rapidly growing community. The student body is a heterogeneous mixture of Anglo-Saxon, Chicano, Asian, and Black students. The approximately 2000 students are taught by a faculty of 80 teachers, most with ten or more years of experience.

The Teachers

This experiment was made easier by the uniqueness of the situation at Irvington High School. All of the biology, four sections with a total of 136 students, is taught by me and my long time friend, Harry Stookey. We have similar academic backgrounds and interests. We both possess California General Secondary Teaching Credentials. We have both taught for twenty-six years. We were both evaluated by the same administrator this year, Mr. Richard Guidici, Vice Principal, and given the same rating—excellent. We are both the same age. The probability of finding a situation where the teachers involved are so closely matched seems unlikely. It provides a unique opportunity for a controlled educational experiment.

The essential difference between me and Harry Stookey is that I have published some freelance writing and attended a five week Invitational Workshop sponsored by the Bay Area Writing Project at the University of California, Berkeley.

The Students

A profile of the biology classes was made to determine what differences existed between the composition of my classes and Harry Stookey's. We were able to obtain the student scores for the Fremont Unified School District Competency Tests and used the written language skill and the reading comprehension scores, along with other data, to construct the profile (see Figure 1).

Apparently my students had slightly lower ability in both written language skills and reading comprehension. They also tended to miss class more often and were younger, as indicated by year in school, than Harry Stookey's classes. They did, however, turn in a higher percentage of their assignments.

Design of the Study

The Problem

Do secondary biology students learn and retain fundamental principles of biology better in a biology program which stresses expressive writing than in a class that uses only traditional expository writing?

Group	Average Score—Written Language Skill	Average Score—Reading Comprehension	Percentage of Assignments Turned In	Average Days Absent Per Pupil	Number of Students Enrolled
Tierney I	85.5	88.5	92	7.6	69
Stookey II	89.5	90.3	87	4.2	67

Figure 1. Comparison of Basic Skills, Assignments Turned In, and Attendance of Groups.

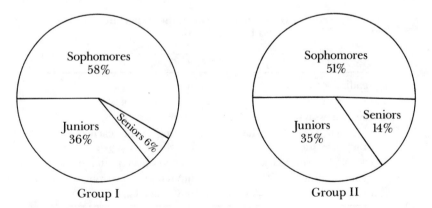

Figure 2. Composition of Groups by Year in School

The Hypothesis

The act of writing encourages a personal response by the student. He [or she] must assume a chosen position, he must involve himself in the subject—he must think. Expressive writing allows him to think in his own language, to sort out what he does know from what he is still confused about, and to do so without intimidation from a teacher-examiner. It seems reasonable that students who have been encouraged to use expressive writing as a vehicle to transport themselves through the "think" part of scientific methodology will not only learn more, but will retain what they have learned to a greater degree than those students who have not used expressive writing to sort out their thoughts.

The Procedure

My two biology classes (69 students) were designated as Group I. Harry Stookey's two classes (67 students) were designated as Group II. The students remained with the same teacher for the entire year. Group I served as the experimental group during the first semester while Group II served as control. The roles of the groups were reversed for the second semester. Thus each teacher served as director of an experimental group and a control group. We hoped this procedure would negate the teacher as a variable in the experiment.

Both experimental and control groups covered the same biology topics at the same time, did the same labs, watched the same educational films, and had homework assignments corrected with a stress upon proper word usage and spelling.

The differences between the experimental group and the control group are shown in the following chart:

**Procedural Differences Between the Experimental
and Control Groups**

Experimental Group	Control Group
1. reading logs	1. no reading logs
2. neuron notes	2. no neuron notes
3. practice essays	3. no practice essays
4. writing to a specific audience other than the teacher	4. writing to the teacher as an examiner
5. end of class summaries	5. no end of class summaries
6. group writing	6. limited group writing
7. essay tests	7. multiple-choice tests

Two units were selected as "test units," i.e., subject matter to be tested and the results compared. The test unit for the first semester was genetics. Genetics was selected because it was scheduled far enough into the semester to allow time to acquaint the students with the writing techniques to be used. The unit was three weeks long. A pretest (multiple-choice) was given just before the Thanksgiving holiday on November 24th, prior to starting instruction about genetics. A posttest (the same multiple-choice test) was given after the unit, on December 19th, just before the Christmas holiday. On April 10th, 16 weeks after the completion of the genetics unit, a recall test (the same multiple-choice test) was given to determine how much of the genetics unit had been retained by the students.

Although we used essay tests as an additional way of utilizing writing to learn in the instruction of the experimental group (see pp. 156–58) multiple-choice tests were used instead of essay for pre- and posttesting of both groups for the following reasons: (1) most standardized tests are multiple-choice and most of our questions came from textbook exams; (2) essay tests may not have been fair to the control group; (3) most biology classes use multiple-choice tests.

The test unit for the second semester, when Harry Stookey's class served as the experimental group, was seed plants. The pretest was given on April 17th. The students took the posttest on May 8th. The recall test was given to the students on May 29th, three weeks after the unit had been completed. Since the school year was about to end we were unable to extend the period between post and recall examinations any longer than three weeks.

The expressive writing exercises used by the experimental groups, and the results of those exercises, are described below.

The Reading Logs

Reading Logs were assigned in an effort to improve reading comprehension and provide opportunity for expressive writing. The students were instructed to record their thoughts, on notebook paper, as they read, as some people do in the margins of books. The notes were to be thoughts or impressions, they were not to be an outline of the reading. The students knew the teacher would not read their Reading Logs. When due, the students held up their Reading Logs to show that they had been completed and then filed them in personal folders which were kept in the classroom but were available to the students at any time.

An anonymous poll of student reaction to the Reading Logs was taken in mid-March. The students were told to rate the value of Reading Logs on a scale of zero to ten on which zero represented "of no value at all" and ten represented "extremely valuable." The reactions of the students, after some initial groans and mumblings about more homework, was mixed. The following scale represents the average value given to the Reading Log by each of the groups:

```
   0     1     2     3     4     5     6     7     8     9     10
   ├──┬──────┬──────┬──────┬──┬┬──┬──────┬──┬┬──┬──────┬──┤
                           Group II            Group I
                           (Stookey)           (Tierney)
```

Some of the anonymous student comments appear below:

> I think the reading log is very useful if you have to write about the chapter then your going to read it. If you write a paragraph or two of something you just read, then it stays on your head a lot longer then just reading it and forgetting it.
>
> —A student in Group I

> The RL was a pain mainly because I ended up doing them one hour or so before they were due. For the most part I would say they weren't helpful to me because of unwillingness to do them before class and consequently I merely rushed to get them done and not fully understanding what I read or wrote. Admittedly they are a good idea, but they shouldn't be used as an assignment because students will BS their way through them. I believe they should be used as an extra-credit, or very carefully read. In this way they would be fully effective.
>
> —A student in Group I

> I think they are great. They are sort of a reward for studying. Not because they are worth five points, but because they help you where you need it most, on the test.
>
> —A student in Group II

> The reading logs don't help at all for me. I think they make reading the chapter harder because you have to stop and right down stuff.
>
> —A student in Group II

The Neuron Notes

Many professional writers keep daily journals. The British seem to have success with "Learning Logs."[2] It sounded like an excellent idea. We called our version of writing-to-think *Neuron Notes*. The Neuron Notes provided another opportunity for expressive writing and forced the student to organize his thought, to sort out what he learned from what he was confused about.

The students were instructed to take at least ten minutes each day to sit down and attempt to explain, to themselves, what they had learned in biology that day. They were encouraged to write down any thoughts that occurred to them even if they regarded the thought as trivial or non-sense. They were also encouraged to pose questions for the teacher about things that confused them. Though Neuron Notes would not be read by the teacher without student permission, we hoped that many students would use them as a vehicle for individualized instruction.

Although 90% of the students wrote Neuron Notes, only a few granted permission to have them read; most of those were regurgitations of what had been presented—not what was actually learned. They were expressed in a style designed to please the teacher. Most students were unable to overcome the idea of writing for a grade.

A few excerpts from Neuron Notes follow:

> Today, we watched a movie on genetics. Considering it was an old movie, it was pretty interesting. It explained how the genes are passed on from generation to generation through heredity. It talked about Mendel's work and how he came to be the father of genetics.
>
> The most interesting part was when it showed the different stages of mitosis. I have a clearer view of how mitosis works by being able to see the changes from interphase to metaphase, etc.
>
> It's also possible for scientists to actually see the genes lined up on a chromosome of a fruit fly. They know this because when a certain gene wasn't present, that trait didn't show up.
>
> —A student in Group II

> I guess I didn't understand the punnett square as well as I thought I did. The thing I don't understand is if it's stated that something is homozygous does that mean that it's dominant or recessive? I'll ask Mr. T. what that means.
>
> —A student in Group I

> We watched a movie about genetics. It showed the idea of our book in different ways. If somebody did not already know what was going on it would be hard to follow. I followed it pretty well.
>
> —A student in Group II

> They explained about Mendel's experiment and I would explain it again on paper but I've written about it so many times I know it by heart.
>
> —A student in Group I

> In biology today we first took a quiz. It was based on what we learned yesterday: monohybrid and dihybrid crosses. I missed problem one all together. I didn't miss it because I didn't know the way to work it. I missed it because I got nervous and confused a little because it was in word problem form. It was asking about the cross of a black heterozygous pacing horse with a black heterozygous

trotting horse. I misread heterozygous as homozygous. The result was that my missing the whole problem, wow was I ever mad at myself.

—A student in Group I

An anonymous response to Neuron Notes was solicited from the students in mid-March, the same day they evaluated the Reading Logs. A rating of zero indicated the students thought Neuron Notes had no value. A rating of ten indicated that Neuron Notes were invaluable as a learning device. The average rating of Neuron Notes by each group is shown on the scale below:

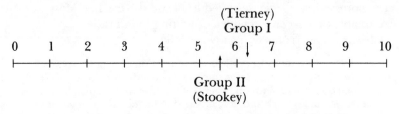

Some written response to the evaluation of Neuron Notes follows:

To say quite honestly I never gave the Neuron Notes a fair chance. A lot of times I wouldn't get them done so I couldn't really say if they would have helped me or not but I did feel they were a good idea.

—A student in Group II

I thought the Neuron Notes were beneficial to me during the genetics part of the course. They made me sit down and determine what I learned and if I was confused to go back and review or ask Mr. Tierney. I think they should be required through other phases of biology. Why can't we do them all year?

—A student in Group I

Neuron notes had a great effect on my learning habits. If I remember what I did each day and can explain it, I usually remember more, and more clearly.

—A student in Group II

The neuron notes helped me some but not as much as the Reading Logs did. Somedays you wouldn't learn anything so you would just put a lot of bull down. I was never that enthused about the neuron notes so I just did it half assed all of the time.

—A student in Group I

The Practice Essays

Science teachers often ask students to write essay-type responses or reports, but seldom take any time to explain to the student how to write one. We mistakenly assume that teaching essay writing is solely the task of the English teacher. We expect the student not only to know how to respond in essay style, but we ask him to write his response without any prior "warmup" or "think-it-through" time. We then correct the student's paper as if it were a final draft, forgetting that few professional writers write a finished piece on the first try.

The teacher assigning an essay should write an essay response to his own question before assigning it to the students. He should allow sufficient time for the student to think through the problem. Since examinations for the experimental group were essay type (except for the objective tests used for research purposes), we tried to provide instruction and practice in essay writing. We called this instruction *Practice Essays.*

The students were told to read the topic carefully and to make any notes they wished, i.e., make a short Reading Log. The students then shared their notes with each other and deleted or added items. Some students volunteered to read their notes aloud; other students were allowed to add items to their own lists. They were then given twenty minutes to write about the topic. They were told it was a first draft and not to be concerned about spelling, grammar, or mechanics. A few of the papers were read aloud for class reaction and comment. The Practice Essay sessions usually took place about a week before the actual exam.

When polled later 75% of the students thought that Practice Essays were very helpful, especially in learning how to take an essay exam. Negative reactions came from about 15% of the class while 10% had no opinion. A few anonymous comments follow (all from Group I):

> I think the practice essay helped me alot. I think it is a very wise study habit. If I were to not write a practice essay I would probably do worse. After I write the practice essay I read it to myself and write things down or rewrite things that I forgot or just needed to make more sense. The practice essay helps alot!

> I feel it is much better to do such a practice SA is a very good idea. Wow this doesn't mean I enjoyed, no way. It was, as I suspected, hard work, but considering it is the first time I have received an A in any kind of science test (at least for as long as I can remember) I feel any amount of hard work is worth it (up to a point).

> I would like to admit something that I never would admit to classmates. Instead of feeling nervous only about the test, for a strange reason I felt it a challenge. I feel it to be a good idea.

> The practice essay was very great! I learned the material much better and it still stays with me. I've learned more by practice essay than by just failing the test. I don't fail the tests since we have practice essays. The class is not boring like most classes are.

> I think the SA test was a waste. I would rather read a chapter out of the book because you can get more information. While writing up the SA you just don't absorb all information.

Writing for a Specific Audience

British studies indicate that 87% of all student writing in science is written to the teacher as an examiner[3]—informing the already informed. It was no great surprise to see that our students were writing to the same audience despite frequent suggestions not to do so. Grade-conscious students feel compelled to tautologize what the teacher has told them, or to write reports that sound like, and often are, copies from the textbook or encyclopedia.

Our alternatives to writing to the teacher as an examiner included: (1) letting the student write to himself as much as possible (Reading Logs and Neuron Notes); (2) having the student write for his peers (group labs); (3) having the student write to the teacher as a partner (Neuron Notes that students asked the teacher to read); (4) having the student pretend to write to a particular person other than the teacher.

The fourth method was accomplished by placing a large photo, or poster, on the wall and asking the student to write for the person depicted on the poster. Sometimes the students wrote for Miss Piggy, Wonder Woman, Evel Knievel, a clown, a boy on a skateboard, a bum in a doorway, an old lady on a porch, Superman, and so on. There were frequent discussions regarding how much the person in the poster might be expected to know about a particular subject. Wonder Woman, it was agreed, probably knew everything, but Miss Piggy would not be expected to know, or care, about the respiration cycle of a cell. These discussions turned out to be excellent review sessions.

The following are excerpts from papers written to a boy on a skateboard. The subject is mitosis and meiosis. Teacher comments follow each excerpt.

> I'm going to explain meiosis to you buddy. It starts out with one cell, with a nuclear membrane. The first stage is that the membrane disintergrates and chromosomes are visible, two more chromosomes are duplicated, and line up right next to each other, then they start twisting up to mix up the genes. All of them line up on the equater and then split into two cells, each carrying two chromosomes, then those two split up again forming four more cells, each have four cells which have one chromosome. This is called haploid.

TEACHER COMMENT: This student starts by addressing the poster, but quickly slips into writing to the teacher as an examiner. His view of what takes place in cell division is a bit distorted.

Mitosis is a term that applies to the splitting of all cells higher than bacteria and not including sex cells. In mitosis the nuclear membrane (a thin wall that covers the nucleus, the control center of the cell) is broken down and distributed throughout the cell. Next the chromosomes of the cells (chromosomes are the bodies in the nucleus that control what you will look like, do, etc.).

TEACHER COMMENT: This student makes an attempt to explain some of the terminology to the boy on the skateboard.

Dear Young man on the skateboard:

I am going to try to explain about mitosis and meiosis. Mitosis is a process that happens when all cells duplicate themselves except sex cells. It starts when the cell nucleus starts dissolving and the chromosomes are present. They duplicate themselves and turn so that they are horizontal with the poles. Then they begin to split and half go to one pole and half to the other pole. The cell then makes a duplicate of itself.

TEACHER COMMENT: This is the voice of a high school biology student attempting to clarify the idea in his own terms. It's reasonably accurate, but probably confusing to his reader.

There are three methods of cell division. One of them is fission and the others are mitosis and meiosis. Mitosis occurs in more advanced cells, and meiosis occurs only in sex cells. In mitosis there are several stages the cell goes through before it divides to form two cells exactly like it. In meiosis, the cell goes through various steps to form four cells. Mitosis and meiosis both involve chromosomes.

TEACHER COMMENT: This sounds like expressive writing that takes place as the student tries to clarify the idea to himself. He's learning.

Mitosis is the splitting up of a cell with a full set of chromosomes. Mitosis can split up all higher level of cells except sex cells. Sex cells are split up by a process called meiosis.

TEACHER COMMENT: The student has grasped one idea, but has ignored his reader and is writing to the teacher.

I'm sorry to tell you that I was sleeping during the lecture and did not have a thing to write. However you should get enough information from the other people that are writing to you, if they know anything. Please do not read this letter while skateboarding or when your doing anything else. Please disregard this letter, burn it up, or throw it away just get rid of it.

TEACHER COMMENT: Refreshingly honest. The student is writing to the skateboarder, but is also apologizing to me for not paying attention. It tells me something about the student and/or my ability to lecture.

I can't explain mitosis very well for I don't understand it yet, myself. But I will try to attempt to explain meiosis. Meiosis is a process in which sex cells are produced. If you have one cell which has 46 chromosomes inside of it the chromosomes split up in half.

TEACHER COMMENT: A confused voice, but being able to admit you don't know is the first step toward learning something. It also informs me that I had better review the subject with the entire class.

End of Class Summaries

Sometimes, after a teacher presentation, the students were asked to take the last fifteen minutes of class to summarize what they had learned about the topic presented. This activity was similar to Neuron Notes except that the student turned it in for credit. The student received full credit if he did it, regardless of content or how well written, and zero credit if he did not turn it in.

Besides an additional opportunity for expressive writing, it provided a real insight into how much of the teacher presentation is being absorbed. It also keeps the class alert and can provide a break in routine.

The following are examples of student summaries after a discussion of cell respiration, a difficult and not very exciting topic:

I don't understand this stuff.

I understand most of what happens in respiration. One thing I don't understand though, is where the carbons go when you lose one or two. Also, where does the $CO_2 + H_2O$ come from when you lose carbons?

What I know about respiration is that all organisms need it. The carbon from glucose is taken and split in two. You take one of the two and it is split into two carbons, the one carbon is used to make CO_2 and H_2O comes out, also. Those were the first steps or the anaerobic stage, it needs no oxygen and happens outside the mitochondria. The aerobic stage needs oxygen and happens in the mitochondria. The mitochondria forms 4C which combines with the 2C. They form 6C. It's split into 5C, carbon forms CO_2 and H_2O.

Sometimes the end of class summary provided an insight different from what was perceived by observing the class. They may all have looked as though they understood, but the summaries often revealed they did not. We knew when we had to cover the material again.

Group Writing

Group writing took place when students worked as a team while doing a lab. Sometimes the team consisted of two students, sometimes three.

Only one paper was required from the group so the writing effort was a team product. We kept everyone honest by occasionally giving an unannounced quiz immediately after the lab was turned in. Students who worked at understanding the lab were rewarded; those who didn't do their share generally lost points.

Another type of group writing occurred when we organized the class into teams in order to solve a problem. Harry Stookey and I, over the years, have developed several group problem-solving assignments. One that was used during this experiment involved trying to determine why the oxygen curve on a lake in San Francisco did not drop very much during the hours of darkness.

We organized the students into teams, taking care to distribute the talent, and presented them with the problem and the data available. As a team they had to formulate a hypothesis, interpret the data, and make some conclusions. They were given parts of several days in class. They also met frequently outside of class. They were told, at first, that each of them must write a first draft and attempt to solve the problem. Later they would get together and review and discuss each other's papers. Then, as a team, they wrote a report that was turned in for grading.

The sharper students seem to enjoy these assignments. There is generally good discussion and cooperation between students in a team, but sometimes one student may dominate the others, resulting in the paper being written by the most grade-conscious student in the team.

There are many biological principles that enter into the problem posed, and the exercises are generally excellent for reviewing material, stimulating ideas, giving students some problem-solving experience, and teaching the nature of science. On occasion the students might argue with our interpretation of a correct answer, and that makes it an interesting challenge for both teachers and students.

Designing one of these assignments is a stimulating experience. It's a chance to be creative. Unfortunately it takes lots of time and time is scarce.

Essay Examinations

All examinations for the experimental group were essay type except the tests given to evaluate the experimental test units (genetics for Group I; seed plants for Group II).

Several days prior to the examination the students were given practice essay instruction and had a good idea about what might be asked.

The following questions are typical of the essay questions asked:

A. *Describe Francisco Redi's experiments.* Remember to: state his problem; his hypothesis; his procedure, including the control used; his results; his conclusions.

B. *Briefly summarize the various hypotheses concerning the development of life on earth. Select one hypothesis and defend or refute it.*

C. *Explain, in as much detail as you can, how the leaf of a plant is adapted for photosynthesis.* Remember what is required for photosynthesis and be sure to explain how the structure of the leaf is suited for these requirements.

In order to evaluate the examination, we first wrote the essays ourselves in order to make certain we looked for particular things and did not reward the glib student who wrote well, but didn't really know the material. Our essay also served as a model for student appeal when the tests were returned. We read our essay to the class, and if some student thought we'd made a mistake on his grade he challenged us by reading his essay aloud. After a discussion, his grade might be altered, either up or down. The discussions were often lively and generally involved the entire class. I thought they became one of our best learning situations. For fun, I kept score on the blackboard, labelling the scoreboard as "NEAT TEACH" and "PUNKS." If the student lost a point I placed a score under "NEAT TEACH." If the student won a point it was credited to the "PUNKS." Although keeping score was designed for fun, it served to eliminate some student reluctance in challenging the authority of the teacher. The students invariably scored more points than the teacher, and they looked forward to the test reviews. Their eagerness motivated me to return their tests as promptly as possible.

Generally speaking the students complained bitterly about essay examinations at first. They often reminded me that biology was not supposed to be an English class. It was interesting, and very satisfying, to hear them ask for essay examinations when my group became the control for the experiment and started using multiple-choice tests.

The essay examination requires a lot of work on the part of the teacher, but we felt it more truly reflected what the students knew about the subject. It rewarded those who prepared. It's also another way to teach writing in the biology class.

Results

The results of the test units (see graphs, pages 164–65) were, for the most part, expected. The pretest for both units, genetics and seed plants, indicated that the previous subject matter knowledge of both control and experimental groups was about the same. The results of the posttests were disappointing, though not unexpected. Since Group II seemed to have more maturity and scored higher on basic skills tests, we expected them to do slightly better than Group I. It was hoped, however, that the writing efforts of Group I might compensate for the difference in basic ability between the two groups. Apparently it didn't. Post-exam results for both experimental test units were very close.

The recall tests, given sixteen weeks after the first unit and three weeks after the second, did, however, indicate a clear difference between experimental and control groups. The experimental groups scored noticeably higher on recall than the control groups.

Conclusions

Apparently students in classes where expressive writing is stressed will score about the same on a particular unit multiple-choice examination as students who are not in a class that emphasizes expressive writing. "School-wise" students learn to memorize what they need to know for a particular test. It would be interesting to see how the groups would have scored if essay tests had been used to evaluate the two units used for comparison in this experiment.

The results of this experiment clearly indicate that students who have been given an opportunity to use expressive writing as a learning tool will retain more of what they have learned.

Although the experiment was not designed to evaluate improvement in student writing, we feel that student writing did improve. If nothing else, students became aware that what they learn in their composition classes does apply in other segments of the curriculum. Another experiment, to assess writing improvement, should be developed and carried out.

It seems clear to us that biology teachers who stress expressive writing will work harder, have a heavier paperwork load, and will have to delete some biology topics from their program to allow time for writing. They will probably derive more satisfaction from their teaching experience, however. Their students will learn the subject matter presented more thoroughly, and their papers, reflecting what the student actually understands, will be more interesting to read. The teacher will be able better to assess his own performance and enjoy the satisfaction of seeing his students learn the principles of biology, improve their basic writing skills, and enjoy the class.

Results, Multiple-Choice Pre, Post, and Recall Test—Genetics

(Based upon mean average test scores expressed in percent correct)

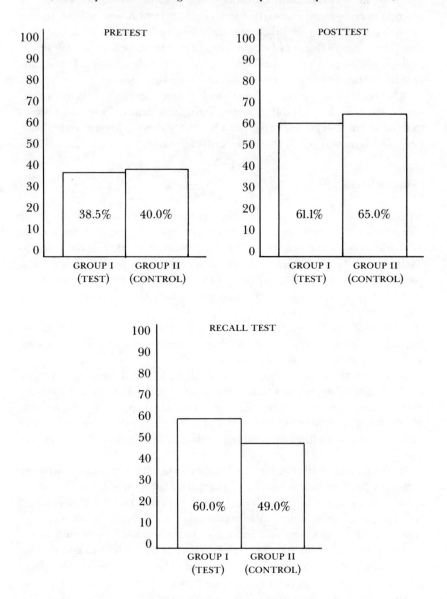

Results, Multiple-Choice Pre, Post, and Recall Test—Seed Plants

(Based upon mean average test scores expressed in percent correct)

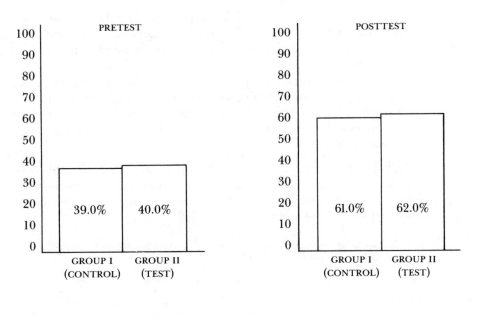

PRETEST

	GROUP I (CONTROL)	GROUP II (TEST)
	39.0%	40.0%

POSTTEST

	GROUP I (CONTROL)	GROUP II (TEST)
	61.0%	62.0%

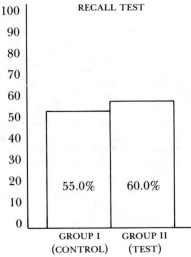

RECALL TEST

	GROUP I (CONTROL)	GROUP II (TEST)
	55.0%	60.0%

Harry Stookey and I, impressed by the results of this experiment, will continue to use the expressive writing techniques cited in this paper with the following modifications:

1. Neuron Notes will not be assigned every day and they will be read by the teacher. We will not correct the papers, but will attempt to carry on a written dialogue with the student to increase his understanding of the subject.
2. The Neuron Notes activity, used in combination with End of Class Summaries, has a lot of potential for individualized instruction. We will continue to refine and develop this technique by increasing the number of End of Class Summaries and decreasing the number of Neuron Notes.

Perhaps what Harry Stookey and I have accomplished with this experiment is a pilot study that may stimulate others to experiment. We certainly gained some valuable insights into our own teaching methods; it was worth our time and effort.

From *Two Studies of Writing in High School Science,* ed. Ann Wotring and Robert Tierney. © 1981 Bay Area Writing Project. Reprinted by permission.

Notes

1. To differentiate the "writing for learning" utilized for the purpose of this study from the usual forms of expository writing required in biology classes, I have adopted the functional categories described in Nancy Martin, et al., *Writing and Learning Across the Curriculum 11–16* (London: Ward Lock Educational, 1976), pp. 22–23. Briefly, they define *transactional writing* as writing "in which it is taken for granted that the writer means what he says and can be challenged for its truthfulness to public knowledge; . . . the language most used in school writing." *Expressive writing,* by contrast, is more like written-down speech, writing in which the writer "feels free to jump from facts to speculation to personal anecdote to emotional outburst and none of it will be taken down and used against him." It is this latter sort of writing we encouraged students to use as a learning tool in our classes.
2. *Writing in Science, Papers from a Seminar with Science Teachers.* London: Schools Council Publications, 1976.
3. *Ibid.*

Bibliography

Allen, R. "Written English as a Second Language." In *Teaching High School Composition*, ed. G. Tate and E. Corbett. New York: Oxford Univ. Press, 1970.

Aristotle. *Rhetoric and Poetics*. Trans. W. Rhys Roberts. New York: Modern Library, 1954.

Atwell, Nancie M. "Class-Based Writing Research: Teachers Learn from Students." *English Journal* 71 (Jan. 1982): 84–87.

Austin, John L. *How to Do Things with Words*. Cambridge: Harvard Univ. Press, 1962.

Bartholomae, David. "The Study of Error." *College Composition and Communication* 31 (Oct. 1980): 253–69.

Bateman, Donald, and Frank Zidonis. *The Effect of a Study of Transformational Grammar on the Writing of Ninth and Tenth Graders*. Champaign, Ill.: National Council of Teachers of English, 1966.

Bateson, Gregory. *Steps to an Ecology of Mind*. New York: Ballantine Books, 1972.

Beers, James, and Edmund H. Henderson. "A Study of Developing Orthographic Concepts among First Graders." *Research in the Teaching of English* 11 (Fall 1977): 133–48.

Berliner, David, et al. *Proposal for Phase III of the Beginning Teacher Evaluation Study*. San Francisco: Far West Laboratory for Educational Research and Development, 1976.

Berlo, David K. *The Process of Communication: An Introduction to Theory and Practice*. New York: Holt, Rinehart & Winston, 1960.

Bernstein, Ruby, and Bernard Tanner. "The California High School Proficiency Examination: Evaluating the Writing Samples." Berkeley: Bay Area Writing Project, Univ. of California, 1977.

Bever, T.G. "The Influence of Speech Performance on Linguistic Structures." In *Advances in Psycholinguistics*, ed. G.B. Flores d'Arcais and W.J.M. Levelt. Amsterdam: North–Holland, 1970.

————. "Perception, Thought, and Language." In *Language Comprehension and the Acquisition of Knowledge*, ed. John Carroll and Roy Freedle. New York: Halsted Press Division of Wiley and Sons, 1972.

Bloom, Benjamin S. *Human Characteristics and School Learning*. New York: McGraw-Hill, 1976.

Bloom, Benjamin S., J. Thomas Hastings, and George F. Madaus. "Learning for Mastery." In *Handbook on Formative and Summative Evaluation of Student Learning*, ed. Benjamin S. Bloom, et al. New York: McGraw-Hill, 1971.

Bridwell, Lillian S. "Revising Strategies in Twelfth Grade Students' Transactional Writing." *Research in the Teaching of English* 14 (Oct. 1980): 197–222.

167

Britton, James, Tony Burgess, N. Martin, Alex McLeod, and H. Rosen. *The Development of Writing Abilities (11–18)*. London: Macmillan, 1975.

Broadhead, Glenn J., James A. Berlin, and Marlis Manley Broadhead. "Sentence Structure in Academic Prose and Its Implications for College Writing Teachers." *Research in the Teaching of English* 16 (Oct. 1982): 225–40.

Brooks, Phyllis. "Mimesis: Grammar and the Echoing Voice." *College English* 35 (Nov. 1973): 161–68.

Brown, Marshall L., and Elmer G. White. *A Grammar for English Sentences, Vol. 1 and 2*. Columbus, Ohio: Merrill, 1968.

Brown, Penelope, and Colin Fraser. "Speech as a Marker of Situation." In *Social Markers in Speech*, ed. Klaus R. Scherer and Howard Giles. Cambridge: Cambridge Univ. Press, 1980.

Bruner, Jerome. "From Communication to Language—A Psychological Perspective." *Cognition* 3 (1974–75): 255–87.

Caplan, Rebekah, and Catherine Keech. "Showing-Writing: A Training Program to Help Students Be Specific." Berkeley: Bay Area Writing Project, Univ. of California, 1980.

Carroll, John B. "Vectors of Prose Style." In *Style in Language*, ed. Thomas A. Sebeok. Cambridge: MIT Press, 1960.

Chafe, Wallace, "The Development of Consciousness in the Production of Narrative." In *The Pear Stories: Cognitive, Cultural, and Linguistic Aspects of Narrative Production, Vol. 3*, ed. Wallace Chafe. Advances in Discourse Processes Series, ed. Roy O. Freedle. Norwood, N.J.: Ablex, 1980.

Cherry, Roger D. "Cohesion and Textuality: A New Perspective on the Development of Writing Ability." Paper presented at the annual meeting of the Conference on College Composition and Communication, Washington, D.C., March 1980.

Chomsky, Noam. *Aspects of the Theory of Syntax*. Cambridge: MIT Press, 1965.

Christensen, Francis, and Bonniejean Christensen. *Notes Toward a New Rhetoric: Nine Essays for Teachers*. 2d ed. New York: Harper & Row, 1978.

Cicero. *De Oratore*. Trans. H. Rackham. 2 vols. Cambridge: Harvard Univ. Press, 1942.

Cole, Michael, and Barbara Means. *Comparative Studies of How People Think: An Introduction*. Cambridge: Harvard Univ. Press, 1981.

Cook-Gumperz, Jenny, John Gumperz, and Herb Simons. "Language at School and Home: Theory, Methods, and Preliminary Findings." Univ. of California, Berkeley, 1979.

Cooper, Charles R., Robert Cherry, Rita Gerber, Stefan Fleischer, Barbara Copley, and Michael Sartisky. "Writing Abilities of Regularly Admitted Freshmen at SUNY-Buffalo." University Learning Center and Graduate Program in English Education, SUNY, Buffalo, 1979.

Cooper, Charles R. "Holistic Evaluation of Writing." In *Evaluating Writing: Describing, Measuring, Judging*, ed. Charles Cooper and Lee Odell. Urbana, Ill.: National Council of Teachers of English, 1977.

Crowhurst, Marion. "Syntactic Complexity and Teachers' Quality Ratings of Narrations and Arguments." *Research in the Teaching of English* 14 (Oct. 1980): 223–31.

D'Amico, Deborah. "Becoming an Author: Second and Third Grade." In *Classroom Experiences,* ed. Naomi M. Gordon, 24–48. Exeter, N.H.: Heinemann, 1984.

D'Angelo, Frank J. *A Conceptual Theory of Rhetoric.* Englewood, N.J.: Winthrop, 1975.

Daly, John A., and Michael D. Miller. "The Empirical Development of an Instrument to Measure Writing Apprehension." *Research in the Teaching of English* 9 (Winter 1975): 242–56.

Davidson, Melissa. "Audience in Student Writing." Classroom Research Project for the Secondary Credential Program of the Bay Area Writing Project, Univ. of California, Berkeley, 1979. Photocopy.

Davis, Barbara, M. Scriven, and S. Thomas. *The Evaluation of Composition Instruction.* Inverness, Calif.: Edgepress, 1981.

Davis, Ken. "The Cloze Test as a Diagnostic Tool for Revision." In *Revising: New Essays for Teachers of Writing,* ed. Ronald A. Sudol. Urbana, Ill.: ERIC/RCS and National Council of Teachers of English, 1982.

Dawson, Melissa. "Changing the Audience in Student Writing." Classroom Research Project for the Secondary Credential Program of the Bay Area Writing Project, Univ. of California, Berkeley, 1979. Photocopy.

DeFord, Diane. "Young Children and Their Writing." In *Theory into Practice* 19, no. 3 (1980): 157–62.

Diederich, Paul B. *Measuring Growth in English.* Urbana, Ill.: National Council of Teachers of English, 1974.

Dore, John. "Conversational Acts and the Acquisition of Language." In *Developmental Pragmatics,* ed. Elinor Ochs and Bambi Schieffelin, 339–61. New York: Academic Press, 1979.

Dunca, Michael, and Bruce Biddle. *The Study of Teaching.* New York: Holt, Rinehart & Winston, 1974.

Duvall-Flynn, Joan. *Writing for Reading: Will Resistant Readers Teach Each Other?* Berkeley: National Writing Project, Univ. of California, 1983.

Dyson, Anne Haas, and Celia Genishi. "'Whatta Ya Tryin' to Write?' Writing as an Interactive Process," *Language Arts* 59, no. 2 (Feb. 1982): 126–32.

Edson, Lee. "The Advent of the Laser Age." *New York Times Magazine,* 26 March 1978, 34.

Elley, W.B., I.H. Barham, H. Lamb, and M. Wyllie. "The Role of Grammar in a Secondary School English Curriculum." *Research in the Teaching of English* 10 (Spring 1976): 5–21.

Emig, Janet. *The Composing Processes of Twelfth Graders.* Urbana, Ill.: National Council of Teachers of English, 1971.

Fillmore, C. "The Need for a Frame Semantics within Linguistics." In *Statistical Methods in Linguistics.* Stockholm: Skriptor, 1976.

Fillmore, Charles. "The Case for Case." In *Universals in Linguistic Theory,* ed. E. Bach and R.T. Harms. New York: Holt, Rinehart & Winston, 1968.

Fisher, R.A. *The Design of Experiments.* 7th ed. Edinburgh: Oliver & Boyd, 1960.

Flanders, Ned A. "Teacher Influence in the Classroom." In *Interaction Analysis: Theory, Research and Application,* ed. E.J. Amidon and J.B. Hough. Reading, Mass.: Addison-Wesley, 1967.

Flower, Linda S., John R. Hayes, and Heidi Swarts. *Revising Functional Documents: The Scenario Principle.* Document Design Project Technical Report no. 10. Pittsburgh: Carnegie-Mellon Univ., 1980.

Flower, Linda S., and John R. Hayes. "The Pregnant Pause: An Inquiry into the Nature of Planning." *Research in the Teaching of English* 15 (Oct. 1981): 229–43.

Freedman, Sarah Warshauer. "The University and the Classroom Teacher: Research Partners." Paper presented at the annual meeting of NCTE, Washington, D.C., November 1982.

Frye, Northrop. *Anatomy of Criticism.* Princeton, N.J.: Princeton Univ. Press, 1957.

Gage, N.L. "Paradigms for Research on Teaching." In *Handbook of Research on Teaching,* ed. N.L. Gage, 118. Chicago: Rand McNally, 1963.

Goswami, Dixie. "Teachers as Researchers." In *Rhetoric and Composition,* ed. Richard Graves. Montclair, N.J.: Boynton/Cook, 1984.

Graves, Donald H. "An Examination of the Writing Processes of Seven-Year-Old Children." *Research in the Teaching of English* 9 (Winter 1975): 227–41.

——. "A New Look at Research on Writing." In *Perspectives on Writing in Grades 1–8,* ed. Shirley M. Haley-James. Urbana, Ill.: National Council of Teachers of English, 1981.

Gray, James, and Robert Benson. "Sentence and Paragraph Modelling." Berkeley: Bay Area Writing Project, Univ. of California, 1982.

Gray, Stephanie, and Catherine Keech. "Writing from Given Information." Berkeley: Bay Area Writing Project, Univ. of California, 1980.

Groff, Patrick. "Children's Spelling of Features of Black English." *Research in the Teaching of English* 12 (Feb. 1978): 21–28.

Grossman, Alberta. "What Happens When Mickey Writes? Reading Between the Lines." In *Research in Writing: Reports from a Teacher-Researcher Seminar,* 115–32. Northern Virginia Writing Project, George Mason Univ., 1982.

Halliday, M.A.K. *Language as Social Semiotic.* Baltimore: University Park Press, 1978.

Halliday, M.A.K., and Ruqaiya Hasan. *Cohesion in English.* London: Longman, 1976.

Herman, Jerry. "The Tutor and the Writing Student: A Case Study." Berkeley: Bay Area Writing Project, Univ. of California, 1979.

Higgins, John. "Teaching the Central Idea—An Inductive Approach." *English Record* 26, no. 4 (Fall 1975): 80–84.

Hill, Ada, and Beth Boone. *If Maslow Taught Writing.* Berkeley: National Writing Project, Univ. of California, 1982.

Hirsch, E.D., Jr. *The Philosophy of Composition.* Chicago: Univ. of Chicago Press, 1977.

Holbrook, David. *English for Maturity.* Cambridge: Cambridge Univ. Press, 1961.

Howgate, Lynn. *Building Self-Esteem through the Writing Process.* Berkeley: National Writing Project, Univ. of California, 1982.

Hunt, Kellogg. *Grammatical Structures Written at Three Grade Levels.* Research Report no. 3. Champaign, Ill.: National Council of Teachers of English, 1965.

Hymes, Dell. *Foundations in Sociolinguistics: An Ethnographic Approach.* Philadelphia: Univ. of Pennsylvania Press, 1974.

International Association for the Evaluation of Educational Achievement. "International Study of Achievement in Written Composition: Scoring Guides," January 1983. Photocopy.

Isaac, Stephen, and William B. Michael. *Handbook in Research and Evaluation.* San Diego, Calif.: EdITS, 1981.

Jakobson, Roman. "Linguistics and Poetics." In *Style in Language,* ed. Thomas Sebeok. Cambridge: MIT Press, 1960.

James, William. *Principles of Psychology.* New York: Dover, 1890.

Katz, Jerrold J., and Paul M. Postal. *An Integrated Theory of Linguistic Descriptions.* Cambridge: MIT Press, 1964.

Keenan, Eleanor. "Why Look at Planned and Unplanned Discourse?" In *Discourse across Time and Space,* ed. E.D. Keenan and T.L. Bennett. Los Angeles: Department of Linguistics, Univ. of Southern California, 1977.

Kinneavy, James L. *A Theory of Discourse.* Englewood Cliffs, N.J.: Prentice-Hall, 1971.

Krashen, Stephen D. "On the Acquisition of Planned Discourse: Written Language as a Second Dialect." Paper presented at the Claremont Reading Conference, Claremont College, Claremont, California, 1978.

Krejcie, R.V., and B.W. Morgan. "Determining Sample Size for Research Activity." *Educational and Psychological Measurement* 30 (1970): 192–93. Reprinted in William B. Michael and Stephen Isaac, *Handbook in Research and Evaluation.* 2d ed. San Diego, Calif.: EdITS, 1981.

Kuhn, Thomas S. *The Structure of Scientific Revolutions.* 2d ed. Chicago: Univ. of Chicago Press, 1970.

LaBerge, David, and S. Jay Samuels. "Toward a Theory of Automatic Information Processing in Reading." *Cognitive Psychology* 6 (1974): 293–323.

Labov, William. "The Transformation of Experience in Narrative Syntax." In *Language in the Inner City: Studies in the Black English Vernacular.* Philadelphia: Univ. of Pennsylvania Press, 1973.

Labov, William, and David Fanshell. *Therapeutic Discourse: Psychotherapy as Conversation.* New York: Academic Press, 1977.

Lakoff, Robin. "What Can You Do with Words: Politeness, Pragmatics, and Performatives." In *Papers from the 1972 Austin, Texas Conference on Performative Speech Acts.* Berkeley and Los Angeles: Univ. of California Press, 1977.

Lane, Kenneth, Sandra Murphy, and Kathleen Berry. "The Writing of the Sophomore Class at Oakland High School." Instructional Research Laboratory, School of Education, Univ. of California, Berkeley, 1981.

Lanham, Richard A. *Revising Prose.* New York: Scribner's, 1979.

Lillya, Terry. "Classroom Investigation of the Teaching of Writing." Classroom Research Project for the Secondary Credential Program of the Bay Area Writing Project, Univ. of California, Berkeley, 1979. Photocopy.

Lloyd-Jones, Richard. "Primary Trait Scoring." In *Evaluating Writing: Describing, Measuring, Judging,* ed. Charles R. Cooper and Lee Odell. Urbana, Ill.: National Council of Teachers of English, 1977.

Loban, Walter. *Language Development: Kindergarten through Grade 12.* Urbana, Ill.: National Council of Teachers of English, 1976.

Macrorie, Ken. *Searching Writing.* Rochelle Park, N.J.: Hayden, 1980.

Marashio, Nancy, and Center School's Eighth Graders. *Writing: A Window to Our Minds.* Berkeley: National Writing Project, Univ. of California, 1982.

Maslow, Abraham, *Motivation and Personality.* New York: Harper & Row, 1954.

Matsuhashi, Ann. "Pausing and Planning: The Tempo of Written Discourse Production." *Research in the Teaching of English* 15 (May 1981): 113–34.

Mehan, Hugh. *Learning Lessons: Social Organization in the Classroom.* Cambridge: Harvard Univ. Press, 1979.

Mellon, John C. *Transformational Sentence Combining: A Method for Enhancing the Development of Syntactic Fluency in English Composition.* Research Report no. 10. Champaign, Ill.: National Council of Teachers of English, 1969.

———. "Issues in the Theory and Practice of Sentence Combining: A Twenty-Year Perspective." In *Sentence Combining and the Teaching of Writing,* ed. Donald A. Daiker, Andrew Kerek, and Max Morenberg, departments of English, the Univ. of Akron and the Univ. of Central Arkansas. Selected papers from the Miami University Conference, Oxford, Ohio, 1978.

Meyer, Bonnie J.F. "Reading Research and the Composition Teacher: The Importance of Plans." *College Composition and Communication* 33 (Feb. 1982): 37–49.

Miles, Josephine. *Working Out Ideas: Predication and Other Uses of Language.* Berkeley: Bay Area Writing Project, Univ. of California, 1979.

Miller, Alyce. "Are Readers Really Writers?" Classroom Research Project for the Secondary Credential Program of the Bay Area Writing Project, Univ. of California, Berkeley, 1980. Photocopy.

Miller, George A. "The Magical Number Seven, Plus or Minus Two." *Psychological Review* 63 (1956): 81–97.

———. *Spontaneous Apprentices: Children and Language.* Minneapolis, Minn.: Winston, 1980.

Mitchell-Kernan, Claudia. "Signifying and Marking: Two Afro-American Speech Acts." In *Directions in Sociolinguistics,* ed. John J. Gumperz and Dell Hymes. New York: Holt, Rinehart & Winston, 1972.

Moffett, James. "Rationale for a New Curriculum in English." In *Rhetoric: Theories of Application,* ed. Robert M. Gorrell. Champaign, Ill.: National Council of Teachers of English, 1967.

———. *Teaching the Universe of Discourse.* Boston: Houghton Mifflin, 1968.

Moffett, James, and Betty Jane Wagner. *Student-Centered Language Arts and Reading, K–13: A Handbook for Teachers.* 2d ed. Boston: Houghton Mifflin, 1976.

Mohr, Marian. "The Teacher as Researcher." Network Newsletter, National Writing Project, Univ. of California, Berkeley, 1980.

Moore, Fernie Baca, and Robert J. Marzano. "Common Errors of Spanish Speakers Learning English." *Research in the Teaching of English* 13 (May 1979): 161–67.

Mullis, Ina V. *The Primary Trait System for Scoring Writing Tasks.* Denver: National Assessment of Educational Progress, 1975.

Myers, Miles A. *The Speech Events Underlying Written Composition.* Ph.D. diss., Univ. of California, Berkeley, 1982.

———. "The Encoding Strategies Used by High School Writers at Different Levels of Competency." Paper presented at the NCTE Spring Conference, Seattle, Washington, April 1983.

Myers, Miles A., and Susan C. Thomas. *The Interaction of Teacher Roles in the Teaching of Writing in Inner City Secondary Schools*. NIE final report (400-80-0024), 1982.

National Assessment of Educational Progress. *Writing Achievement, 1969–1979: Results from the Third National Writing Assessment*. Vol. 1, *Seventeen-year-olds*. Vol. 2, *Thirteen-year-olds*. Denver: National Assessment of Educational Progress, 1980.

Nixon, Jon. *A Teacher's Guide to Action Research: Evaluation, Enquiry, and Development in the Classroom*. London: Grant McIntyre Limited, 1981.

O'Hare, Frank. *Sentence Combining: Improving Student Writing without Formal Grammar Instruction*. Research Report no. 15. Urbana, Ill.: National Council of Teachers of English, 1973.

Odell, Lee, and Dixie Goswami. "Writing in a Non-Academic Setting." *Research in the Teaching of English* 16, no. 3 (Oct. 1982): 201–23.

Olson, David R. "From Utterance to Text: The Bias of Language in Speaking and Writing." *Harvard Educational Review* 47 (Aug. 1977): 157–81.

Osgood, Charles E., G.J. Suci, and Percy H. Tannenbaum. *The Measurement of Meaning*. Urbana, Ill.: Univ. of Illinois Press, 1957.

Perl, Sondra. "The Composing Process of Unskilled College Writers." *Research in the Teaching of English* 13 (Dec. 1979): 317–36.

Piaget, Jean, and Barbel Inhelder. *The Psychology of the Child*. New York: Basic Books, 1969.

Pianko, Sharon. "A Description of the Composing Processes of College Freshman Writers." *Research in the Teaching of English* 13 (Feb. 1979): 5–22.

Posner, M.I., and C.R.R. Synder. "Facilitation and Inhibition in the Processing of Signals." In *Attention and Performance 5*, ed. P.M.A. Rabbitt and S. Dornic. New York: Academic Press, 1975.

Rogers, Carl R. *Client Centered Therapy*. Boston: Houghton Mifflin, 1951.

Rommetveit, Ragnar. *Words, Meanings, and Messages: Theory and Experiments in Psycholinguistics*. New York: Academic Press, 1968.

Rubin, Donald L., and Gene L. Piche. "Development in Syntactic and Strategic Aspects of Audience Adaptation Skills in Written Persuasive Communication." *Research in the Teaching of English* 13 (Dec. 1979): 293–316.

Schank, Roger C., and Robert P. Abelson. *Scripts, Plans, Goals, and Understanding: An Inquiry into Human Knowledge Structures*. Advance papers of the Fourth International Joint Conference on Artificial Intelligence, Thilisi, Georgia, U.S.S.R. Hillsdale, N.J.: Lawrence Erlbaum Associates, 1977.

Schulman, Lee S. "The Missing Paradigm in Research in Teaching." Lecture presented at the Research and Development Center for Teacher Education, Austin, Texas, 1984.

Searle, John. "Indirect Speech Acts." In *Speech Acts*, vol. 3 of *Syntax and Semantics*, ed. P. Cole and J.L. Morgan, 59–82. New York: Seminar Press, 1975.

———. *Speech Acts*. London: Cambridge Univ. Press, 1969.

Shaughnessy, Mina P. "Basic Writing." In *Ten Bibliographic Essays*, ed. Gary Tate. Fort Worth: Texas Christian Univ. Press, 1976.

———. *Errors and Expectations: A Guide for the Teacher of Basic Writing*. New York: Oxford Univ. Press, 1977.

Shepherd, Lawrence. "An Examination of the Writing Assignments at Skyline High School, May 1982." Classroom Research Project for the Secondary Credential Program of the Bay Area Writing Project, Univ. of California, Berkeley, 1983.

Sherwin, J. Stephen. *Four Problems in Teaching English: A Critique of Research.* Scranton, Pa.: International Textbook Company for the National Council of Teachers of English, 1969.

Siegel, Gail, Lynda Chittenden, Jean Jensen, and Jan Wall. "Sequences in Writing, Grades K–13." Berkeley: Bay Area Writing Project, Univ. of California, 1980.

Simon, Herbert A. *The Sciences of the Artificial.* 2d ed. Cambridge: MIT Press, 1981.

Smith, William L. "The Effect of the Structure of Topic on Students' Writing." Paper presented at the NCTE Spring Conference, Seattle, Washingon, April 1983.

Stanovich, Keith E. "Toward an Interactive-Compensatory Model of Individual Differences in the Development of Reading Fluency." *Reading Research Quarterly* 16 (1980): 32–71.

Strong, William. *Sentence Combining: A Composing Book.* New York: Random House, 1973.

Takala, Sauli, Alan Purves, and Annette Buckmaster. "On the Interrelationships between Language, Perception, Thought and Culture and Their Relevance to the Assessment of Written Composition." *Evaluation in Education: An International Review Series* 5, no. 3 (1982): 317–42.

Tierney, Robert. "Using Expressive Writing to Teach Biology." In *Two Studies of Writing in High School Science,* ed. Ann Wotring and Robert Tierney. Berkeley: Bay Area Writing Project, Univ. of California, 1981.

Wiley, Beth. "A Comparison of Reading Test Scores and Writing Ability." Classroom Research Project for the Secondary Credential Program of the Bay Area Writing Project, Univ. of California, Berkeley, 1983.

Williams, Joseph. *Style: Ten Lessons in Clarity and Grace.* Glenview, Ill.: Scott, Foresman, 1985.

Williams, Joseph M. "Defining Complexity." *College English* 40 (Feb. 1979): 595–609.

Williams, Laurie. "A Protocol Analysis of a Fourteen-Year-Old." Classroom Research Project for the Secondary Credential Program of the Bay Area Writing Project, Univ. of California, Berkeley, 1979.

Williams, Patty Sue. "Four Ways First Graders Revise." *Research in Writing: Reports from a Teacher-Researcher Seminar,* 196–205. Fairfax, Va.: Northern Virginia Writing Project, George Mason Univ., 1982.

Winters, Lynn. "Alternative Scoring Systems for Predicting Criterion Group Membership." Paper presented at the annual meeting of the American Educational Research Association, San Francisco, April 1979.

Winterowd, W. Ross. *The Contemporary Writer: A Practical Rhetoric.* 2d ed. New York: Harcourt Brace Jovanovich, 1981.

———. "The Grammar of Coherence." In *Contemporary Rhetoric: Conceptual Background with Readings,* ed. W. Ross Winterowd. New York: Harcourt Brace Jovanovich, 1975.

Witte, Stephen P., and Lester Faigley. "Coherence, Cohesion, and Writing Quality." *College Composition and Communication* 32 (May 1981): 189–204.

Yamagishi, Miki. "Sentence Modelling and Its Effectiveness on Student Writing." Classroom Research Project for the Secondary Credential Program of the Bay Area Writing Project, Univ. of California, Berkeley, 1980.

Ylvisaker, Miriam. *An Experiment in Encouraging Fluency*. Berkeley: Bay Area Writing Project, Univ. of California, 1979.

Index